Dedicated to: Isabel, who I will now see grow up (I hope!)

Raising money for: The Midlands Air Ambulance Charity, and awareness for NHS Blood Donation.

With thanks to: The Ambulance Service, Cheltenham & Gloucester Fire Services, Gloucestershire Police, Air Ambulances from Great Western and Midlands, Southmead Hospital, Royal Gloucester Hospital, The Winfield Hospital, Ken Goodwin @ ITV, The Dowdeswell Estate contractors, and all of my family and friends without whom I wouldn't have been able to do this

Life is all about choices...we all have choices, and we all have to take responsibility for those that we make.

No one makes us think how we do, behave as we do, feel as we do....except us ourselves.

It's a hard concept, but once you get your head around it life becomes much easier.

I had a choice on Thursday 12th July 2018, that was very apparent to me - both at the time, and since then.

But never more than at the time....

To breathe or not to breathe...

The car was spinning, round and round, across the road....and I wasn't breathing.
I know I wasn't breathing because I could see myself...weird as that sounds.
When I stop spinning I'll breathe....

The car stopped spinning eventually, after what felt like an eternity....
And I still didn't breathe.
I had to tell myself to breathe....fucking breathe....

My biggest choice in life....
If I hadn't breathed, I'd be dead now.

CHAPTER 1
Life can change in an instant

Pre 12th July 2018 – life was good

I got divorced this year. Well, my ex (Pete) and I actually split up in October 2016, but it's taken that long - quickie divorces definitely do not exist!

So life has been pretty up and down for a significant time.

We have a 4 year old daughter together. "4 and a half" I hear her yelling at me. Actually, by the time I've finished this, she'll probably be nearer 5!

Life has been tricky, but you persevere don't you? Again, a choice for us all. Don't get me wrong, there have been days that I've been in all sorts of a mess. In fact, those are the days that I've stayed in bed...and there have been a lot of those! But there have been good times too, plenty of those as well.

In fact, a good time was just starting. Iz and I had just moved into our little 3 bed semi in Cheltenham. Specifically, in Charlton Kings – schools are brilliant there you see, and Iz starts this year (2018). Our house was fantastic, but needed a lot of work doing to it, and it was ours...all ours to do what we liked with. We loved it. We only got the keys mid June, and then headed on holiday for a week in Crete with Grandma. We got back on the Tuesday night and I then went on a hen do in Barcelona on the Thursday early doors. Katy (my cousin) and Kieran get married in September so we're seeing her into it in style with a few days in the sunshine.

Anyway, we all got back from the hen do on the Saturday night, late.

Sunday was a right off - for obvious reasons!

So – by Wednesday - life is manic, boxes are still everywhere, house is a tip......you get the picture?

Neil, my partner, and I went to the local pub on the Wednesday night to watch England lose the football to the Czech Rep in the World Cup semi finals. We had dinner there and a couple of beers. We were home and in bed by 2300 (pretty early for us, but I had a new job starting the next day so I was attempting to be responsible!)

So life was good (except for England losing...that's not so good!)

Thursday 12th July 2018 - Life can change in an instant

I was to start a new contract today...Freixenet. So excited to be working with them - my next 12 months were sorted, or so I thought.

Work sorted, income sorted, extension on house sorted, holidays sorted etc..

The handover was planned in Thame for 1030 so I needed to be on the road just after 0900. I was meeting Sam, and we were having coffee and cake. Sam is finishing to have a baby so she'll definitely want cake!

0910 - I left my house at the same time as Neil. He went one way towards Gloucester and I went the other, towards Oxford.
I remember driving down East End Road, and turning onto the A40 by the service station in Charlton Kings.
And that's it, no proper memory after that of my (apparently very short) journey. In fact, if you ask me now I'll still say that I think I was further down the road than I actually was!

The car was spinning, round and round and round and round....I wasn't breathing.
I know I wasn't breathing because I could see myself...weird as that sounds to anyone who is reading this.
When I stop spinning I'll breathe....
The car stopped spinning eventually, after what felt like an eternity....
And I didn't breathe.

I had to tell myself to breathe..."fucking breathe"....

And that was it...my most significant choice in life. If I hadn't consciously chosen to breathe then, I'd be dead now.

Dead.

I breathed. And then I looked out of my window. I saw the other car on the other side of the road, what looked like miles away. And I reached for my phone to call the police.

And then the weird feeling. My middle felt odd. Best way I can describe it I'm afraid - just not right.

People started collecting around the cars. Running between the two of us. It felt like most of them were with the other car at the start.

I remember asking the guy how long it would be before help arrived, and he said he could hear them. I think I must have blacked out then as I don't remember anyone actually arriving or talking to me initially.

I remember people desperately trying to get my door open, but it was jammed. Airbags were in my face, but someone got rid of them.

This amazing man suddenly appeared behind (but next to, if that makes sense) me in my car. I remember telling him that there was clearly something wrong with my right foot....not sure what gave me that impression....maybe the foot being at least 20cm from the ankle? And something felt odd about my middle. I told him my left foot was fine (another joke for later).

I also remember him taking my watch and asking if he should put it in my bag...yes please.

Then I must have been in and out of consciousness.

I remember the fire brigade cutting various parts of the car and glass shattering. They used boards to protect me and whoever was with me. I remember them telling me exactly what they were doing at all times. To be honest, I didn't really care. I trusted them implicitly to get me out and make sure that I was ok in the process.

I remember them trying to cut the bonnet twice, and the car getting closer and closer to my knees... I felt it crush both times and screamed.

After that I don't remember clearly. I say clearly like I remember clearly before..."clearly" in relation to before!

I literally must have been in and out of consciousness. I dreamt that I was free from the car and the paramedics were running me through the fields to the helicopter.

I believe I was given ketamine (explains a lot) by the Air Ambulance crew that I now know were there.

Apparently I had 2 blood transfusions at the scene. One given from Midlands Air Ambulance, and one given by Great Western Air Ambulance. I have no recollection of either. I've been told this since.

2 Air Ambulances...I've not seen that before. Not that I saw it this time either!

I woke up at the point of being dragged from my car - I think the dragging was more from necessity than the car being ready for me to come out from. I remember the fire brigade and ambulance getting tense with each other at this point. I also remember telling them to just get me out and leave my legs behind - I think I had started to panic now.

I was trapped for over 1.5hours. The cut off for anyone is an hour. By rights, again, I shouldn't be here.

Running through the field....the air ambulance men, not me. I was, for once in my life, being carried!

And I got to go in a helicopter!! Not quite the ride I had hoped for, or imagined. But a helicopter nonetheless!

Hmmm – it probably would have helped if I'd been awake throughout and able to appreciate it! I was definitely in and out of consciousness.

But I do remember 3 lovely doctors with me. And ladies, it is like the programmes....

Men – the ladies will know exactly what I mean!

I must have been the most annoying passenger ever, like a child.

I remember asking twice "are we nearly there yet?" It could only be improved by the reply being "just around the next corner".

But the 2nd reply was actually even better – "I can see the hospital in the distance". Thank God.

I had pads around my head, and a neck brace on. My 2 worst nightmares.

I get claustrophobia you see. I'm really not good at being "trapped" in any way, shape, or form.

I think a man came and helped my trolley into the emergency room, but again I think I was in and out of consciousness.

In the ED room there were so many people and lights everywhere.

All around me.

You only see this in Holby or Casualty right?

No, it happens in real life. Except that it hurts a lot more than watching the TV.

And you're thirsty. Really thirsty.

But you can't have anything, because they want to check you first.

They wanted to find out where my bleeding was so that they could assess whether or not they would operate on me immediately.

My first question I think when I came around and was at a form of reality level – "is the other driver ok?"

Apparently he was also in the ED room – less than 20m from me. And he was "ok" ish....alive.

He was in for CT before me.

I remember being hot, very hot. A lovely lady kept wetting towels and putting them around my forehead and neck.

But I still had these bloody pads on either side of my neck. And I remember trying to get them off.

I was irritable. I now know that this indicates internal bleeding and can be a thing they look for in patients. The more irritable, the more bleeding. I was seriously irritable.

I asked for Neil. He was there – thank goodness. I didn't even think about how he was there. But he was there.

He held my hand. Bless him, I don't know how he held it all together, but he did. He had my bag from the car too. It's the simple things in life. Again, I didn't ask how. I was just glad that he was there and he had my things.

I remember him asking me when he should phone my mum, but I wanted to wait until we knew more. I still don't think I was taking things quite as seriously as I should have been. I think I was actually thinking that we might not need to worry my mum at all - stupid really!

I finally went for my scans....out of consciousness again. But maybe they did this on purpose! It's got to be easier to scan people who lie still!!

Once my scans were done I remember being allowed some water through a straw for the first time. It felt like the best thing on the planet. It must have been at least 1500 by this point, and I left home at 0900. I was parched!!

It was also at this time that the police took the opportunity to breathalyse me. I genuinely had no issue with this, and remember it. I would never drink and drive, let alone at 0900 in the morning!

And then I was moved to the Intensive Care Unit... again, absolutely no recollection.

You could be forgiven for thinking this was a good thing. But really, it's not. What it actually meant, in hindsight, was that I was too broken to operate on immediately. I needed to be stabilised.

I do have a vague recollection of FaceTiming my friend Katy….she had had a couple of wines, and I was high on drugs…great combo. I wanted to let her know that I didn't think (in hindsight this is hysterical) that we'd make it to theirs this weekend.

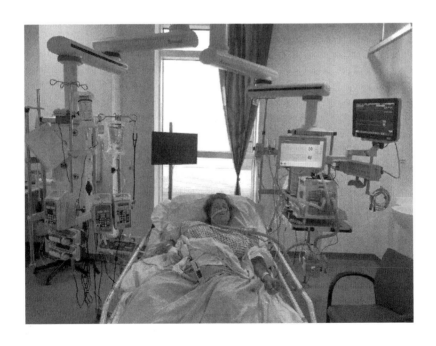

From Neil - that day:

"After seeing England lose in the World Cup semifinals on Wednesday 11th July, I had no idea how Emily's, Iz's, and her mums life was going to change. Oh, and mine. Unusually we did not drink that much the night of the football and ended up in bed by 2300. Partially because of Em's new job starting the next day.

The morning of the 12th went quickly after getting up and dressing etc for work. We both left Emily's house a little after 0900 with a quick peck on the cheek after having a little argument the night before, and with not many cuddles due to time we parted on good terms.

I was in work a little after 0930, the usual late time for me. A little before 1030 I had a call on my mobile from an unknown number. A man who announced he was calling from the police control room asked me to confirm my name and whether I was insured to drive a black Audi A4 estate to which I replied no. He asked me if I was insured to drive an Audi Q5. Thinking this could be a bogus caller as he got the information wrong first of all I asked him to prove who he was before I told him anything more. He promptly said to call the police control room and gave me a number to dial and said to ask for his name but to hurry. Realising the urgency in his voice I did say I was insured to drive an Audi Q5 and that it was my partners car, Emily. He said that he needed to send an officer round to me and asked me to confirm where I was. I asked him if Emily was ok but he said he couldn't tell me anything but the officer would. I confirmed my work address and he said the officer will be around soon. I immediately called Emily but this went to answering machine, so I left a message asking after her and hoping she was okay. Thinking the police would be about 5 minutes I went outside immediately without telling anyone. I sat outside for 10 minutes on a bench at work next to the pond not knowing what had happened and thinking the worst. I couldn't bring myself to cry at that point. It must have been shock. After about 10 minutes I thought I would go back in the office and gather my stuff because there was no way this was good news. I asked the receptionist and the security officer at the front desk to call me on my mobile when the police turn up. The more I talked the more I could feel myself getting upset, to which I apologised to the receptionist and security guard.

I went back upstairs to my desk and saw Jo, one of my bosses, at her desk. I went up to her desk and couldn't get any words out without crying, so Jo had no idea what was going on. She took me to a seating area secluded from other people and, sobbing, I told about the police calling me. She immediately took me downstairs and outside saying that we were better off outside with no one asking what was going on and am I alright. On the way, I think to clear my desk of rubbish, because I'm leaving the office, and I manage to throw a coffee cup towards the bin but missing the bin and spilling coffee down the leg of one of the architects who was talking right in front of the bin. He actually had a little go at me saying I hope there's no stain down his trousers. I apologised and proceeded to throw the cup in the bin after the 3rd attempt!

I was calmer outside with Jo. She really helped me that day and I will never forget it... I couldn't have had more support from anyone else. Jo and I talked about the reality of the situation and knowing it's not good news, but we don't know if it's the worst news either...trying to keep things in perspective worked but it was the longest 40 minutes of my life!

When the police turned up they explained what had happened to Em. She was being air lifted to Southmead Bristol now and insisted on driving me to Southmead as they could turn the blue lights on should Em's condition worsen and get me there faster.

A fairly long drive but I felt in control holding conversation with both officers and asking questions. Finding out we all knew another police officer, my best mates little brother, helped. Still, a long 35 minute journey, but no blue lights needed at least! Any other time blue lights and siren might have been exciting but I welcomed them not being on!

Went into the trauma unit at approx 1200 and although Emily was there they wouldn't let me see her and couldn't tell me a lot either. She was undergoing scans and X-rays to determine her injuries - more waiting! The looks the staff were giving me were of pity...think they knew something I didn't. Made me feel uneasy. By 1230 the other drivers relatives had turned up...an elderly lady most likely his mum...was crying her heart out...but the police were quick to maintain separation of each drivers relatives. I was the only person there for Em. I had a discussion with the police and agreed that Em's mum, Jane, should not have the same call as I had. I would wait until I knew more of Em's condition and maybe talk to her then. That decision to tell close relatives is a risky one but I felt that sending a police car to Chipping Norton, and Jane waiting that long was too awful and we could handle it better for her. We finally got a side room to wait in.

After a cup of water and another hour I was allowed in to see her in one of the trauma unit bays. Seeing her alive and pretty compus-mentos was surprising and relieving. This compus mentus behaviour of Em's carried on throughout her time in hospital, but at that time I didn't realise that she wouldn't remember a fair amount of what she said. She behaved like she was in charge at times throughout her hospital stay...bless her...but the drugs did provide her with moments of lucid ness.

Emily had 2 orange blocks each side of her head to stop her from moving her head but it was a full time job keeping them in place, Em was feeling claustrophobic.

Em was desperate for a drink...the nurse got water but it took ages to find a straw to enable Em to drink it. Bless the health service! It is the only thing I got slightly frustrated with...I was going to go to the hospital restaurant myself but Em was gripping my hand.

The Consultant explained at about 1415 the extent of her injuries...the first time I had seen Emily cry. I couldn't help but say to her... but you're still here with us...I had to question if I was being condescending but she didn't realise for another 2 days how lucky she had been and close to death she had been. I actually still don't think she's really realised it.

Why would she when shock and drugs were plentiful? The drugs were definitely needed!

Emily asked me where her bag was...the nurse had given it to me. She asked me to look after it. The police had taken her phone. She asked me to keep her rings safe. After that all I remember is Em saying sorry to me. Dozy tart... why say sorry? I was just glad she was alive! She kept saying sorry for the next 2 weeks, she always thinks of others before herself!

Em and I were told that she was being transferred up to the Intensive Care Unit. This was going to happen soon. I was asked to leave them to get on with it. It seemed a very short time to spend with her, finding the straw occupied most of the time. I said I would let her mum know and that she and I would be back later in time for visiting her in ICU. I wondered what lie to tell her mum. I couldn't tell her the truth, not yet.

I went into the side room for some privacy and took some deep breaths. It's not a good trait to be able to lie...but I had to do it. When Jane picked up the phone I hoped I sounded all light and of no worries. It seemed to be working...Jane wasn't talking much but asked questions about Em. We arranged for me to pick her up and bring her to the hospital. The car accident was the truth and a broken leg was the truth, I just left out a few of the other more serious things.

I sent Pete (Izzy's Dad) a message that Emily had been in an accident and could he look after Iz until tomorrow and Jane would be in touch tomorrow morning to work out who Iz stays with for the rest of the weekend.

I called the company that Emily was due to start work with that day explaining what had happened and left my phone number. I knew how crucial this job was for her so promised that I would stay in touch not knowing when she would start work. This job was going to provide her with enough money to pay for her house extension and stop her from diving into her savings to live day to day. I hoped they would keep it open for her.

In the police car on the way back to my work, I worked out that Jane and I were only going to have an hour max with Emily in ICU if I were to pick Jane up from home. The A40 was still closed due to Em's accident but we would get 2 hours if she could meet me at my work, 40 mins away from her. I called Jane again and asked her to meet me at my work.

Arriving back at work at approximately 1540, I had a lot of work people asking how Emily was and they were being so kind and helpful. The programme I was working on had put everyone under severe pressure, some to breaking point. Yet these people could see clearly that the work they had to do didn't really matter compared to what had happened to Emily. It could have happened to somebody they loved too. My boss, who is not the most emotional human being, had offered to pay a taxi home for me if the police couldn't bring me back from Bristol. He also said not to worry about work, the most thoughtful I had seen him EVER!!!
I could see that Em was going to be in hospital for a while and knew that I should be with her. My boys would understand that couldn't spend this weekend with them. Another colleague and friend had offered to look after my boys at the weekend if their mum couldn't.
All the above put my faith back in people and made me feel grateful for knowing them.

Jane called me at about 1630 saying she was at Sainsbury's which was just down the road. By the time I was out of my work she was there. I got in the car and guided her to parking place next to my car. Jane was in fairly good spirits considering. As soon as she and I got into my car I had to tell her everything as there was no way I could tell her on the way or later as I knew we would talk about what I knew about Em's accident etc. I had to tell her before I started driving. She handled it really well. I apologised for not telling her before and gave my reasons. We chatted about Emily for the whole journey.

On arrival we made our way to ICU. We asked reception if we could see Emily. She phoned through to Em's room - yes - private rooms in ICU. The receptionist said to the person on the other end of the phone that Emily's PARENTS were here to see her. I didn't think a lot of it at that point but Emily found it very amusing...and still does! I can say this more because Jane looks young rather I look old! Well I think that anyway.

When we got into her ICU room, Emily had up to 6 NHS staff in her room....the more staff the more serious things are. It must have been most heart wrenching for Jane to see Emily like that. I was surprised too. She had at least 3 machines giving her drugs, loads of monitors which made lots of beeps, and lots of electronic cords attached to her. Seeing Emily lying there made it look even more serious than in the A&E trauma unit. Jane and I found a seat whilst letting the NHS professionals do there jobs.

So, it's 1830, and Emily says..."can you bring my laptop in with you tomorrow and my iPad and can you check with the police when I'm going to get my phone back please? I have clients I need to speak to." I recounted Emily's numerous injuries and how we'd ended up here:
Road Traffic Accident serious enough to be airlifted and resulting in 27 broken bones including a shattered pelvis, lucky to be alive, being given loads of drugs, attention, and care by NHS staff that the Queen would get if she were ill in hospital...and she still wants to work and make sure her clients and other colleagues are ok.
I thought this was the drugs talking...but after hearing the same things most days since her accident...it is just her.

Wow!!!

We were asked to leave at 1900 for 30mins whilst and a handover was given to the night shift. Visiting hours were 1000 - 2000 but the amazing staff let us stay longer until gone 2100. I didn't want to leave her, fearful that her lacerated spleen and her carotid artery were not stable. These were the 2 most serious issues despite everything else and the reason why her broken bones were not operated on for 2 days.

When Jane and I left I said I would stay at Emily's with Jane as it was possible that we would get a *call in the night. OMG I could have done with more than 1 beer that night!!!*

I went to bed at midnight...I had a little blubber and recalled when my dad was in hospital and may not survive the night 23 years ago. I hadn't thought about that for years. I prayed to God back then...but I wasn't going to be such a hypocrite this time, being an Atheist. After all, it's the health professionals looking after Emily that really matter!
Well ... writing this 12 weeks later...those health professionals, their training and the equipment available, oh...and Emily's pure force of will..or stubbornness!!! She's still here, and getting better every day."

"Emily has read my account above. Quite rightly she has asked if I am the same person that she remembers me being on that 1st day that we started seeing each other, and all the days that we have been together. You see, I am normally quite sensitive and in touch with my emotions, much more so than the regular man! I know I have not demonstrated what I went through on that day, emotionally. I do know that I felt extremely upset and a little out of control in the first 30 minutes or so and after hearing that Emily was alive, I thought that "I can't be that emotional" as I would be good for nothing and no good for Emily or anyone. It was a choice. I have only considered this after talking it through with Emily. But I have written a little more about that day…"

"The good news is that I am not an emotional cripple and I am still the same person that Emily thinks I am! What I have come to recognise is how I deal with emotional fallout from significant life events. To try and explain this, my dad suffered a heart attack and stroke over 23 years ago in which his heart arrested 3 times, and this was the first time I realised my parents were not invincible. He is, thankfully, still with us. But over 3 years ago he was diagnosed with Alzheimer's, and we have significant issues to deal with as a family to make sure we do what is best for my dad and mum. I also separated from my boys mother over 2 years ago. I went to court once, and nearly another couple of times, just to get time with my two boys but things have settled down for now, though it has not been easy.

It is only now that I recognise that I have chosen to deal with all these events in the same way as I have Emily's accident. I have chosen to not face into it. If I choose to face into any one of these things I believe I could crumble and certainly for a number of days (hopefully not longer) be useful to no one. I have to ask myself, what would I gain? Everyone goes through shit times and nobody likes to be around somebody who is constantly moaning about their life.

Like Emily has said to me many times; "In life you make choices". My choice is to be thankful for the outcomes of these life events as I have little control over them. I will make sure those around me are looked after when needed, and I will do as much as I can. Life is too fragile...don't mope and dwell too much with your own feelings, it is good to do, but I believe not always good to do for too long. I choose to make the most of life in the time that I have, and I love Emily as much as I can love anyone. I know that much about myself and I am very good with knowing that about myself.
See - I am slightly soppy after all!"

From Mum - How a day can change your life:

"Thursday 12th July 2018, a day etched on my memory for ever.

The day started as "normal", with doing my exercises, having the usual breakfast, getting washed and dressed. Then I started making some plain flapjacks for the Church party in the park the following Saturday.

I was feeling excited about this and looking forward to being part of the fun. The weather forecast was perfect too, not always the case! I finished my flapjacks and made a cup of coffee before heading off to my friend Christine's for lunch. We have become very good friends and both moved to Chipping Norton about the same time. In fact I nearly bought the house Christine is now living in!
We had a lovely lunch sitting out on the terrace in the sunshine, with plenty of chattering, I was completely oblivious to the horrendous events going on that morning.
I headed back home about 1430 having a hairdressers appointment booked for 1600, before heading over to my daughter's in Cheltenham.

My little granddaughter, Izzy, was going to be there and I was thinking about what we could do on the Friday - bounce and play, swimming, or park - all very good fun.
I checked my phone when I got home and noticed a missed call and voicemail from Neil, my

daughter's partner. It did occur to me that this was unusual. I listened to the voicemail which told me that Em had been in an accident but was ok and they were at the hospital in Bristol. I did wonder what Em was doing in Bristol but told myself that she probably had a business meeting. I phoned Neil back and he said he was coming to get me and take me to Bristol so I quickly threw a few clothes in a case, enough for a few days, thinking "oh she'll be out of hospital and home for the weekend". So still oblivious to the seriousness of it all. I phoned Christine and burst into tears and she came straight round and helped me focus on getting a bag together. I also phoned the hairdressers in tears and told them I wouldn't make my 1600 appointment. In the meantime Neil phoned and asked if I could meet him in Cheltenham and we could go from there to Bristol. He also mentioned that the A40 was closed, this is the route I would normally take, but still I didn't link this to what had happened and think I said something like "oh dear another accident". So I headed off to meet Neil at his workplace and was quite proud I managed to find my way there! The first thing I said to Neil was "what was Em doing in Bristol?", to which he responded "ah there is something I need to tell you". So, sitting in his car, he told me how serious the accident had been, the A40 being closed for most of the day, Em being airlifted to Southmead major trauma centre in Bristol. But he reassured me that Em was conscious and ok. She would need surgery though. By this time she had been moved to intensive care. I felt completely numb and rather sick. It was difficult to take it all in. In fact, I'm still processing the life changing events of that day. I just wanted to see my beautiful daughter, give her a big hug and know she was ok, and thought about her going through the trauma of the accident "alone". The drive to Bristol seemed to take forever and I was so grateful that it was Neil with me, he has been so wonderfully supportive and, in hindsight, it was right that he only told me about the accident in detail when I was with him and face to face. I couldn't cry at that point but have cried many times since. Seeing Em with so many tubes and attachments was horrible but I knew she was in the best place and that she would be cared for. The staff were amazing and let us stay beyond normal visiting time. They were constantly monitoring all her many serious injuries, but Em was conscious and very chatty considering what she had been through. Neil and myself were quite subdued on the return to Cheltenham and I didn't sleep that night. I phoned my brother to tell him, we were all in shock.

I have a strong and deep faith, and know the good Lord, along with the wonderfully skilled and caring medics, saved my daughter's life on that day. My Church family have been so supportive, kind and caring, and it is very comforting for me to know that we are all in their prayers and this gives me the strength to carry on supporting my *precious daughter and little grand daughter. Life will never be quite the same again and there are some very low times but I am positive about the future and do believe good will come out of something so horrendous, I still have my lovely daughter.*

I cannot begin to know what she is going through but I do know that I love her and my granddaughter with all my heart and I will always be there for them. I'm very proud of her!"

CHAPTER 2

The days and weeks that followed

13th July 2018 – Ketamine is a horse drug...

Neil and Mum came to visit first thing – 1000 - that's first thing for visitors to a hospital. To be fair, unless you're like me in Intensive Care, you're still getting washed and dressed before then. Obviously in Intensive Care you're not really bothered about these things...and can't physically do them anyway.

They both stayed until 2000. How bored must they have been?!

Apparently, I was talking very quietly still – weakness does this.

I actually don't remember any of this, it's purely what I've been told since then.

What I do remember is that I had a chest infection. I remember having the sore throat a couple of days earlier, and feeling it moving to my chest on the morning of my accident.

Coughing when you've been in a serious accident is the worst thing to try and do. Especially when you're told that you need to try and breathe deeply to ensure it doesn't get any worse. Try this with broken ribs.

Nightmare.

And I definitely remember this. I remember being told to try and breathe in more on numerous occasions. Clearly I paid absolutely no attention to this!

Anyway, apparently Mum and Neil spent most of the morning trying to find out what exactly my injuries were.

I was insistent that I'd be home in 5 days!

Hysterical!!

I remember this vaguely too...

I was also insistent that no one needed to be in to visit me after my main operation tomorrow. Or before.

Neil thought otherwise, thank goodness. I must have been a complete pain in the arse to deal with. I do know that, but it doesn't change me.

Apparently, I'm having a five hour operation tomorrow to fix some metal plates in my right ankle, my pelvis and my right femur.

Ouch.

The good thing is that I can't feel anything at all. I'm on so many drugs that I feel like a complete zombie. I literally just lie in my bed and whisper - a lot!

I do remember calling my ex husband, Pete, to speak to my 4 year old daughter. She was meant to be back at mine last night and I was distraught that she would be wondering what was going on and where her mummy was. She was at her cousins and not remotely bothered about me being on the phone as she was blissfully unaware of the events of the last 24 hours - exactly as it should be. I am eternally grateful for the fact that she has a loving family on both sides.

I also remember that I was drinking out of a sippy cup, with a straw...

You know - the ones that you have when you can't do anything for yourself.

Usually for the elderly.

And I remember my Gran having one for the last year of her life.

Things you take for granted...

And then I called Gill. My bestest friend for 20+ years.

Gill was my first boss after university, and we hit it off straight away. We were also housemates for a couple of years, and we've seen each other get married, have children, and all of them get to the age they are at now. She's seen me through 3 long term relationships, and plenty of heartbreak.

This was something else though.

I actually don't remember this call, I've been told. I called her on Neil's phone, and tried to tell her I'd been in an accident...apparently I was muffled and not comprehensive at all. I'm not sure what she heard but I had to hand the phone to Neil as I was too upset to speak to her. Neil started to tell her my extensive list of injuries, that him and my mum now knew. Poor Gill had to hang up as she was too upset.

You see, Gill and I had kind of lost a bit of our friendship in the past year due to my divorce and things surrounding it. But now that's all out of the window. I needed Gill and she needed me to be ok.

My list of injuries (at this point):

Broken vertebrae x 2

Broken Neck in 2 places

Broken ribs x 3 on right side

Smashed pelvis in numerous places

Smashed right femur

Smashed right ankle

Lacerated spleen

Lacerated Liver

Ruptured Carotid Artery

Most importantly of the day...did you know that it can take 2 hours to prepare ketamine for a human in hospital?

I say in hospital as I'm fully aware that it's used recreationally, and I'm guessing takes nowhere near this time to prepare then!!

My interesting fact of the day! (clearly written in hindsight as I was not capable at 1 day post accident!)

Also - comedy of the day - Neil and my mum are apparently my parents!!

Neil - my dad!!

Ha ha!

Love it!

The receptionist and a nurse so far...comedy!

14th July 2018 – stable at last

My operation lasted from 0800-1800. This was the first opportunity that the professionals have had to do this as I haven't been stable enough so far since the accident. That is terrifying. I don't think about it for too long as it really upsets me.

So - nearly 10 hours of operating, and they still didn't manage my ankle….I have to wait a couple of days for this one as they ran out of time and I have to recover in between.

Mr Acharya is the main man. He came in to operate on me and work his magic on my smashed bones.

Neil and mum were waiting patiently for me when I got back from theatre.

They had come in thinking that I'd be done by 1500. As it was, I wasn't back until 1730…they were waiting and worried, bless them. I can't imagine how hard this must have been.

I woke up to the best response I've seen (smiles and hugs) - I actually think this was more because I felt more coherent than I had since the accident, and I actually think I can remember this reaction!!

In hindsight, it could also have been the general anaesthetic doing this.

So, 6.5 hours of surgery and over an hour in recovery.

Resting and filled with ketamine for pain relief.

Being monitored by numerous machines and 3 members of the amazing care team.

Mum and Neil were thrown out at 2000. I made sure that I told them to eat…"Mum – please make sure that Neil eats and vice versa". Classic really, considering I was the one lying in a hospital bed and not able to do anything for myself.

As an aside, apparently my veins are hard to find. I actually know this from my IVF days. Yes, it becomes "days" after you have several rounds!

So, it took 3 doctors over an hour with numerous tries, and an ultrasound machine to actually find something useable in my hand or arm!

Whoops!

15th July 2018 - writing a text…..hmmm….how long does it take???

Neil and Mum arrived around 1000 as normal. I say "normal" as Intensive Care feels like my new home: I don't move out of the bed (not that I can!!), I know all of the staff by first name, and I don't eat anything except for toast!

It actually feels a little like a hotel. Private rooms and all that. Just a few more machines and tubes.

Today was probably the first day I actually took a bit of notice of my surroundings. I say that like I knew what was going on…I clearly didn't when I look back, and was drugged up to the eyeballs!

I do remember a lady arriving in the room opposite who had 2 prison guards with her at all times. I was desperate to know what she had done…maybe I should focus on myself more?!

Neil couldn't believe that my next operation would be the next day. I hadn't exactly recovered from the one the previous day yet.

And apparently I would be moved to a normal trauma ward post my operation. Seemed a little premature but we'll go with it for now.

I do remember that the pain was horrific.

Actually, horrific wasn't the word.

The drugs from yesterday's operation were wearing off. The general and local anaesthetics were all gone...pain was all I could feel.

Bring on some Morphine please.

That didn't work and they couldn't get my pain under control...

Ketamine again it is.

My learning of today, it takes a phenomenal amount of time to type, and it will always be incorrect, if on Ketamine and Morphine!!

The spelling has to be the hardest!

A classic example of one my Facebook messages is below. It took me at least 30 mins for every message. And I sent lots of these messages....no idea who to though!

Ah - to clarify - the reason for the FB messages... my phone is not with me, and hasn't been since the accident. The police have it as part of the investigation and I can't get it back yet. I'm starting to feel like my arm has been chopped off or something....normally I'd be feeling it after about 5 minutes without my phone, but broken bones and intensive care do this to you. There is a slight delay to this feeling!

Strangely I've not been overly bothered about my phone and other things yet, except for my make up! I look horrific! Ordered new bits already!

The bags under my eyes are worse than ever... they look like suitcases loaded for a month long holiday!

At least there are no spots on my face though, every cloud and all that.

It's at this point, where I mention looks/beauty etc, that I have to reference the fact that when you're in this state, ALL dignity is lost.

And I mean ALL.

You are at the complete mercy of those around you - admittedly they are good people and they are making you better, but when you are lying there and relying on them for everything it's a pretty sobering thought.

Thankfully I only had this thought in hindsight. At the time I couldn't have cared less!

16th July 2018 - dark ages

Excellent - my ankle will be sorted today, and all my body will be put back together as much as possible.

So I was consciously starved from first thing.

No food, no drink. A mere 50ml of water per hour.

Grrrrr.

I asked several times during the day if the operation was still on, but they were insistent that the operation would go ahead today...

We waited until 1630 before finally being told that I was not having my operation today.

Neil kept me company whilst I had toast and marmite. The best toast and marmite I think I've ever had. Maybe my judgement was a tad clouded by the starvation!

Not sure what we did all day in hindsight. I whispered, Neil talked. Apparently I said "sorry" and "pardon" a lot!

Ah - except for my entertainment of the day...

Because the police have my nice new iPhone 8, Neil brought me in another phone to use for the interim.

An iPhone 4.

Brilliant - how things move on in such a short space of time!

To be fair, it's exactly what I need for now. I only need to send and receive texts and calls. I can use my iPad for FaceTime and email.

And I'm definitely not ungrateful. I just found it entertaining.

What I should actually be doing is nothing, but I can't leave my work alone. People need me and what I do. That's the whole point of my business.

17th July 2018 - back into one piece

That operation on my ankle....it's definitely happening - and it's only going to take 1 hour!

Compared to the last operation this is nothing!

And I'm loving general anaesthetics, a proper pro! I actually feel really good after them and not what was expected at all.

It's all relative though. I suspect that if I wasn't hurting so much generally then I'm sure I wouldn't feel quite as good after the general anaesthetic.

When I got back from theatre today, my Aunt (Tina) and Uncle (Peter) were waiting for me in my room. So lovely to see them.

Apparently my friend Sophie went for lunch with Uncle P and Auntie T. Then they came in for half an hour before they had to head back to Maidenhead. I actually feel really chuffed that they came to see me. Bristol is 80 odd miles from Maidenhead and I know they're busy. I must be in a pretty bad way for them to drive over so soon.

Again, quite thought provoking really.

And again, I don't really like to think about this as I'll get too upset.

Sophie came in after they left (only 2 guests at a time allowed) and stayed until 1500ish. She is amazing and the best friend anyone could have. She bought me a box of super practical goodies - face wipes, vaseline, chocolate, shampoo, mints, tweezers etc. Love her. You can tell she has 3 kids, she's super organised in everything! I love the fact that she's so practical too. It must have been hard for her to see me with loads of tubes and wires, but to not show emotion in front of me.

We've known each other since the first year of university. We lived in the same halls of residence in our first year, then shared a house for 2 years, and have stayed close ever since....20+ years. Our kids play together and we drink together - perfect!

Today was slightly different to the norm!

Neil came in later and entertained me for a while. Mum is looking after Iz and taking her to and from preschool etc. Her and Pete are trying to keep things as normal as possible for Izzy.

18th July 2018 - friend therapy

Gill came in to visit me mid morning. It was so good to see her, and super emotional.

See, I haven't seen much of Gill in the last year or so as we had that rocky patch after my divorce.

A good thing is that my accident has definitely wiped all of that and really brought it home that we are friends, and will be for life. It shouldn't take something this serious though.

She also bought in goodies for me from Ethel and Helen (more housemates from a previous life) - bless them. I'm so so grateful as everyone is being really kind. I'm pretty sure I cried a lot.

The physio's came and dragged me out of bed. They don't let you rest at all and, as soon as they can, they get you up and about. I know it's for the best, but seriously...I only had my 2nd operation yesterday!

They arrived whilst Gill was with me and I happily let her stay while they got me up. They actually got me into the chair.

Yay!

So painful. But I did it.

I think I made it for about 20 minutes before howling that I needed to get back to being horizontal in my bed.

I have to say here that all the family and friends that have been to see me so far are what has given me the strength to get up.

The strength to take the broken steps to my chair.

The strength to be upright.

I couldn't have done it without them.

And the amazing NHS - I will probably mention them a lot. They are truly incredible. Always smiling, always there, always on it.

Back to it - I haven't yet mentioned this to you - I can't turn over at all. I am flat on my back 24 hours a day (ha ha!). I have to have 4-6 nurses (male and female) come in and lift me either side 4 times a day. They wash me and change the sheets. It's incredible what they do. I have a whole new perspective on things. I am literally helpless and these amazing people look after people like myself constantly.

I am also horrified at how little they earn.

They deserve medals.

More concerningly than most things, or at least it seems to be to those around me, I haven't pooed yet. I may as well get it out there - the fact that I haven't - not the actual poo!

So, the nurses asked if I wanted a suppository or an enema?

Hmmmm...suppository?...

Who on earth would volunteer to have an enema?? Unless on some retreat for weight loss or something!

Enema is absolutely NOT going to happen.

No way.

Nope.

Suppository didn't work by the afternoon. They gave me another one. This doesn't look good for the enema prospects at this stage.

So the suppository didn't work.

Or did it?

I fell asleep for the night, drugged up nicely.

Uh oh...woke up...worst night ever....pooed the bed...twice! And it was only 2200.

And as if that wasn't enough, I then felt the need to accuse the nurse that was looking after me, and changing my bed, of conspiring with other nurses and patients, to murder me. I seriously thought everyone was out to get me, and that whatever it was that they were pumping into my arm, through the drips, was killing me. I genuinely couldn't move a muscle, but felt that my head was working and the nurse was pumping me full of poison and everyone was there watching me die.

Awful night.

That well known murderous hospital - Southmead!!

I blame the Ketamine, apparently it can have that effect.

It doesn't really make me feel any better about my accusations if I'm honest.

19th July 2018 - 1 week in ITU

When I woke up, I apologised profusely to Nancy...I felt awful for accusing her of trying to kill me last night.

So embarrassed.

I also cannot believe that I pooed in the bed...
although apparently everyone does this!

To be honest, I'm not sure I care that much as the
pain is too great.

At least I haven't wee'd the bed...yet! But that's
probably because I have a catheter and it would
be tricky to actually wee the bed!

Admittedly there's something pretty good about
not having to move at all to go to the toilet
(forget the poo for a minute).

And as a mummy we crave some down time with
nothing at all to do...here it is!!

Anyway, back to serious stuff.

I take a look at my left foot after getting up to
take a few steps again - the physio's literally
never give up, they are evil!

Now, if I was at home and nothing else was wrong
with me (hard to imagine right now as I lie here in
an ITU bed), I'd go to the doctors...something is
not right. It's bruised and swollen.

So I ask a nurse, and get sent for another x-ray. So
much easier than going to the doctors! It's like you
get listened to here, and that you know your own
body!

There's a broken left foot too...marvellous.

Another couple of bones.

Just add them to the total.

So I'm given a boot to wear on my left "good" foot to help me walk…

Back to ITU, all stocked up and ready to walk again (sort of!).

As soon as I got back, I was told I was well enough to move to the trauma ward and they moved me almost straight away. It all happened really quickly.

Before I left, the ITU consultant came to see me…"has anyone told you about your CT scans yet?". Urr, not other than the multitude of injuries that I am already aware of…..

"OK – so you have a cyst on your ovary…your left one, about 4cm"

Great – I'll deal with it when all this has settled down.

Another thing for the list. I'm going to have to get a new page…

I travelled on my flat bed to ward 26B.

I'm actually quite excited about the change.

It was awful.

Whilst they found me a bed, I looked around. It was so busy...especially compared to where I had been.

I got put in a bay of 4 beds. Apparently you get put here because you need more attention from the staff.

I brought down the average age - bonus!

From 91 years to 78.5 years...I'll let you work that out (I'm 42 years old!).

And I got looked at like I had 3 heads by the other 3 patients.

Oh, and they lost all my notes and medication - in the space of 1 floor in the lift.

WTF?!

I was in agony and desperately in need of my medication. Neil was trying to get it sorted and rapidly losing his rag.

Then a nurse came along and removed my morphine drip, saying I clearly didn't need it anymore.

Now, this was a shock as I'd been pressing it all day due to the pain I was in. But, apparently the computer log said I'd pressed it on average once every 4 hours...and clearly they decided that I was lying and that the machine was correct.

Aggghhh, nightmare.

I think I had to restrain Neil by this point...

We compromised on some instant morphine tablets to relieve pain - which I downed at every opportunity.

Neil was hoofed out at the end of visiting hours and I had to lie there and contemplate pain and my new home.

The lights went out and the night began.

20th July 2018 - my new home

Last night was absolutely horrific. I think I actually thought I'd rather die at one point.

No, I didn't really. I just lay crying with despair. I actually don't think I've ever reached "that" point, although I appreciate that people do.

Basically, I was in pain, and no-one was helping me. When I buzzed the nurse, I got a healthcare assistant who just asked me what I wanted.

I'd gone from 1 to 1 care (or 6 to 1 at the very start) to 1 to 4.

I'd gone from being turned 4 times a day/night and having the sheets changed around me, me being washed etc...to nothing.

When I asked the lady about turning me, she just asked if that's what I actually wanted, and then proceeded to try and make me do it myself.

WTF - seriously?! I have no idea what I want...other than to get better! I can't move for f**k sake...I need help!

I also had the poor lady in the next bed imagining that her husband was in bed with her and she was chatting to him all night. Funny in any other scenario, but not when you have no idea what to do with yourself as you just want to get out of somewhere.

By this morning I'd figured out that here I have to ask for everything, whereas in ITU you don't ask it just happens - they predict what you need and you get told. Totally different on a ward.

Ok, so now I know, I can maybe work with it.

Still crying, I called Neil and asked him to come in.

Still in bed.

Still in pain.

But feeling more positive now and more like myself. Different staff too.

I did notice that the lady from the night shift was not allowed in our section again. I think I kicked up such a stink about her from the previous night...

I also called my private healthcare company. I'm paying £85 per month so surely I may as well use it?

Anyway, they were brilliant - maybe because I was balling down the phone to them and begging them to get me out of where I was.

Brilliant....until I asked about getting a room near home...nothing was available for a week.

I cried again.

And again.

I literally didn't know what to do with myself - so I had to pull myself together. Otherwise I'll just be sat crying, and that's not really an option for me.

So - back to it.

2 of the ladies left to go to other hospitals and we got a new lady - Shirley.

Shirley is lovely, and cheeky and funny, and certainly doesn't look her 85 years. Hope I look

that good at that age!
Average age now 74.

Woo hoo - party!!

And it's a Saturday - apparently. I've totally lost track and couldn't tell you!

The physio's came...I hid under the duvet...only joking!

I'm more than happy to get up as I want to get better as soon as I can.

Hmmmm....standing on my left foot with boot (good foot...broken...but good), not easy...and walking was even worse.

I have a mental block for that foot now that it has a boot on it, I can't move it. No matter how many times the physio says "walk normally", I can't.

So the boot gets the hoof!

They even tried a different frame...a really special one for people who have problems from the chest down, so that you can put the weight here instead.

I couldn't do that either. So, the next thing I knew was that they had written "hoist only" on the board above my bed!

The consultants visited today. It's strange to see them in the new environment and not in the life or death scenario that I guess I was in for a while. I actually had to double take to recognise them, sounds odd I know. But actually totally different circumstances and a different location.

They are pleased with my progress and also said that I don't need to bother with the boot on my left foot when I weight bear, as long as I'm not in pain. Thank goodness, because the boot and I were not friends. Hideous thing.

Only thing is that they didn't tell the nurses or physios.

So, my board says "hoist only", and it's the weekend.

No nurse would dare get me out of bed!

Now most of us would be happy with this scenario...but not when you've already been in bed for 1.5weeks. I'm literally crawling the walls.

Oh, bad thing from today - I phoned Pete to ask him to bring Isabel in now that all my tubes have gone and I'm on a main ward. He said "no" as he wasn't sure it was the right environment for her. Now I'm more than supportive of this viewpoint if you're in and out in a day or 2, or you have tubes hanging out of you, but I'm going to be in for weeks. I did point this out, and the fact that "normal" is not going to exist for a very long time

- it's actually taken me a while to think about this too.

I won't ever be the same. Let's not go there now!

So anyway, I asked him to come in on his own. He wanted to know why. I actually thought this was quite obvious - to see that I was ok for our daughter to see. I also pointed out that everyone who had seen me so far had cried as I just look awful and I'd rather he got that out of the way before Iz comes in with him.

A decision was made for him not to come in on his own and we agreed that Izzy would come in with Pete after a party the next day.

So - 12 days since I've seen my baby girl, and I'll finally get to see her again.

Horrendous for a parent, and horrendous to feel so helpless.

You actually have to laugh, otherwise you'll cry.

21st July 2018 - the best

My best day yet.

My usual breakfast of marmite on toast - they know me really well now so I don't even need to ask!

Then I actually put some clothes on.

Let me context this....we're not talking fully dressed, were talking a beach top that's long. Nothing else!

I can't actually get knickers and a bra on. I can't bend down and my top half is too swollen! Attractive! Oh, and there's no way I could put them on myself even if I wanted to!

My mum came to see me in the morning, then Sarah and Paul joined us. Great to see Sarah - albeit on crutches. The last time I saw her, a couple of weeks ago, she'd just had her knee op and was in loads of pain. So it was good to see her back on her feet and smiling.

And they bought me chocolate - love my friends!

The irony of it all is that I was meant to be the one driving Sarah around after her operation. Reality is that she will probably end up doing it for me. Damn it!

They all left before Pete and Iz arrived.

Oh my goodness, it was so good to see my gorgeous little girl. I have no idea how I held the tears in as I've cried every day so far, but I did. Probably because Pete had said so many times about it to me, we should shield Iz from it.

Iz was a superstar and climbed on the bed next to me for cuddles. She knew not to touch my "owies" and was super careful. We watched the iPad together and ate choccies. She even went over and offered one to Shirley, love her.

I love my little girl, and I miss her terribly. It's been 12 days since we saw each other. Too long for any mum and daughter.

You shouldn't have to be without any child for so long, even if you're in hospital.

As I've already said, I felt in a helpless situation, and I sobbed a lot about it. Very very wrong.

The funniest moment - Iz wanted to know what the bag of wee was at the side of the bed. There's no point in lying to her. She's an intelligent kid and can take all the information in. So I told her that mummy has to have a wee wee bag at the moment as I can't get out of bed to go to the toilet. She found that hysterical, especially as her daddy was sitting by the wee wee bag!

But that wasn't enough for her, no surprise there (Suzi - when you read this I know you'll laugh!) ....she wanted to know how the wee got in the bag...so I explained the tube.

But that wasn't enough either..."how does it get in the tube?"

Hmmm - not sure how to actually answer that...so I find myself looking at Pete. Absolutely no help! He says I should answer!! So I just tell her the truth.

The truth always works best!

Neil and his mum came in as soon as Pete and Iz left, nice and chilled. Good to see them both, but I was shattered so they didn't stay long.

Queue guilt of them driving all the way to see me...etc...!

22nd July 2018 - road trip

Woke up and had my usual brekkie of tablets and toast.

I must be rattling by now. I genuinely haven't counted how many tablets I'm taking at the moment - it's got to be in the 40's over the day. I hate taking tablets at the best of times.

Shirley was in lots of pain this morning as her hip had popped out again (yuk!).

Sad to see.

I feel a bit of a hypocrite as I don't feel the need to complain about pain much and look absolutely fine - when lying in a bed and not moving!!

So, this was the day.

I decided to go for it and get them to hoist me out of bed into the chair that was literally 30cm from me in my bed.

Hysterical and mortifying both at the same time!

Apparently all nurses had to try the hoists when they were fitted - this made me feel marginally better. Actually, thank goodness for the 2 young nurses that were on today and just taking the piss the whole time. Probably the best way to do it as

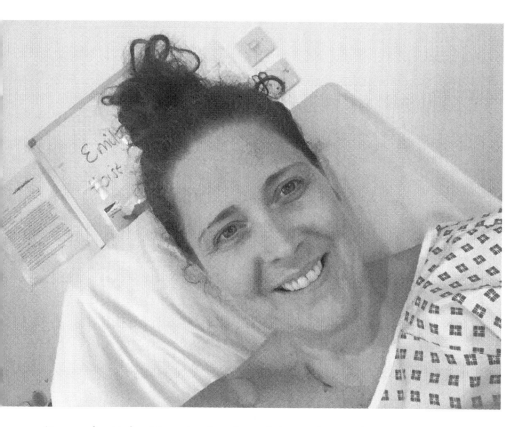

it made it better to be laughing about it. Otherwise I'd probably cry as it's quite horrific when you think about it - I've gone from doing everything for myself, to nothing.

Seriously though....everyone needs a go. It's highly entertaining. I'm sure everyone saw everything, but to be honest I don't care anymore! I've had so many doctors and nurses look at various bits of me that it's really not important in the grand scheme of things.

After moving into the chair, I lasted a grand 15 minutes before needing to be flat again!

Hoist back!

At about 1630 the head nurse came in and told me that I would be moving to Gloucester today, even though there was no bed for me.

Hmmmm??

How's this going to work then?

So apparently, they'd pile me into an ambulance and drive me up there. Then I'd be taken into the ED and admitted through there when they find a bed. Basically they use this method to force a hospital to find a bed. I'm horrified. I'm a patient being transferred to a hospital with no bed. I presume this happens all the time. Awful.

Don't get me wrong, I understand, but what a hideous state for our system to be in.

Neil was on the phone to me and on his way in, so he came in anyway.

Literally 10mins after he arrived, so did the 2 ambulance ladies who were here to take me. They were great fun. I'm off to Gloucester on a flat bed!

Now, this was the first time I saw daylight in nearly 2 weeks. Amazing. I actually saw the hospital too. Its pretty impressive. It reminded me of an airport as it has check in desks and all sorts. The organisation is phenomenal.

I had to ask the girls transporting me to let me enjoy being outside for a few minutes given that it was the first I'd seen since 12th July.

It felt like nothing I can describe, and seriously emotional.

Basic huh?!

After 10minutes in the air, they got me into the ambulance. 45mins and I was at the Royal Gloucester.

Neil followed us in his car, and made sure he had all the paperwork for the drugs etc that I needed as we couldn't afford for a repeat of when I moved to the ward where they lost all the paperwork. I would need my painkillers as soon as I got there so it was critical to have the paperwork.

We got there and managed to bypass the ED room totally.... straight up to ward 2A, and a private room – amazing! I'm seriously lucking out... it's like I have serious injuries or something. Still not really sinking in....

Matt, the nurse in charge, came to see us and make sure I was settled ok.

I needed more drugs but...

wait for it...

no, they hadn't lost the paperwork....

BUT we needed a doctor on call to sign them off....different health authority you see...

Neil was fuming, again! There was literally steam coming out of his ears, and I was in tears, again.

Absolutely unbelievable.

We have a piece of paper in a folder detailing all the drugs needed and when, written and signed by numerous doctors. Yet we need a new prescription from scratch.

Quite frankly I don't care – JUST GET IT SORTED. The pain is so bad.

Once that was sorted (only 2 hours this time) I was good.

And all settled into my new bed for a sleep.

23rd July 2018 - habit

I quite like it here. The nurses are all really friendly, and the brekkie of marmite on toast is good. I'm such a creature of habit...apple juice and marmite on toast - with butter...every morning.

A consultant called Mr Curwen came around today with some students – this was the day that he took me under his wing and said that he would happily have me at the Winfield when I move to private.

Yay! Someone to take me! I can tell WPA at last!

We're all go!

Damn it...Winfield still have no rooms until Thursday....3 more nights...

Oh well, as I said, I quite like it here.

I must say now that Mr Curwen is cool. I met him for all of 5 minutes, and I know already that he swears like a trooper and doesn't like rules.

Love him

24th July 2018 - wee!

New physio's now as I'm in another hospital.

They came to say hi and got me out of bed pretty quickly. I went to the bathroom and back! And then I sat in the chair.

I'll say at this point, that I am only just getting some clothes on each day...because Im forced to! And when I say clothes...I mean a dress, and that's it. I'm still too wounded and swollen for anything else.

It's actually easier on my pelvis if I lie down, so I'm going to get back into bed I think.

Catheter out!! Woo hoo! Oh no, what happens if I wee myself?

When Gill and Sarah came in I had to ask Gill what happens if I wet the bed?! She rightly told me not to be so ridiculous. I'd known before when I needed a wee hadn't I? So surely I'd know now!

OK, mind at ease... sort of.

Gill, Sarah, and I had some lunch together and, more importantly, cakes!

Gill drove them up here and I'm so grateful. I haven't seen Gill this much in ages and it's so nice. Sarah is still on crutches and can't drive so it was lovely to have her here too.

Back to the catheter - what am I going to tell Iz?... she loved the catheter!

More importantly, it was Matt that removed the catheter for me. I can't believe I let him. I literally have no shame left.

I've actually poo'd in the bed since my accident so it doesn't even matter to me that a man has prodded around down there too!

On the poo front - I feel it important for anyone that ever finds themselves in a similar position, and I hope that none of you do...but ,if you happen to find yourself taking 40+ tablets a day, then your system just stops working.

Nothing.

Nada.

And the nurses don't leave you alone! Rightly so, but mortifying!

Rob and Anna came in tonight. It was lovely to see them, although I don't actually feel like I have a lot to talk about.

Accident. That's about it at moment.

Anna deserves a medal. She works in the cardiac unit here at Royal Gloucester. She helps people every day and always has a smile on her face. Huge respect.

Then Neil came in to see me. I feel really bad as he's been at work and then come to see me, but I'm shattered and just want to go to sleep. I cry on him as I feel really guilty that I'm so tired.

But, in amongst my guilt, I do ask him to get us fish and chips...I'm in desperate need of decent(!) food...he goes to the local chippie and brings food back. I eat half of mine...my appetite has shrunk somewhat.

He only stayed half an hour after food as I needed that sleep, and I'm an emotional wreck.

25th July 2018 - cleanliness!

Hair wash day – our healthcare assistants are amazing!

In a shower and everything.

Oh my goodness...what a matt in my hair. It was truly horrific and took about 20 minutes to brush out...I think I lost half my hair in the brush!

I can't tell you how good it was to have a hair wash again though. I'm seriously disgusted with myself and my appearance since 12th July!

More physio...down the corridor this time. All on a frame I must add! These people are robots! But I made sure that I was cheerful, and that I said hello to everyone on my travels.

The people that I'm meeting here are inspirational. Everyone has problems of their own - accidents etc. And they either get on with it or they don't. And everyone that I'm meeting gets on with it. They deal with it in their own ways. I have to point out, that I'm only actually meeting the mobile people...so the people that can or want to help themselves. I have no idea of the split...

People have said that they can't believe how I'm getting on considering what happened. But I don't see it. Not at all. I would never have behaved any differently. And I don't see myself doing anything wonderful, just getting on with it and being me.

Neil was gobsmacked when he saw me on my feet for the first time this evening. And dressed - in the same manner that I mentioned earlier...dress... that's it :)

Here you go - although I do look rough....

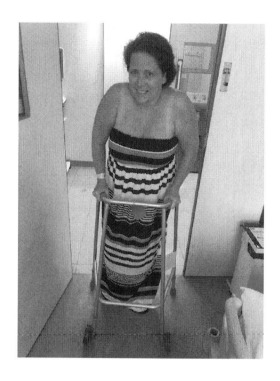

26th July 2018 – private treatment begins

I'm off to The Winfield today! I actually feel quite sad as I've become attached to things here. The staff are amazing and work like dogs, but still have smiles on their faces. It really does put what I do to shame. I just sell food and drink. This is why I've set up Absolute Clarity with Sarah. We want to help people. Ok, so it's not medical, but it's still helping.

Back to my journey to the Winfield....

2 men arrived at about 1300 to transfer me. It's literally only 1 mile. I could walk it if I hadn't lost the use of my legs and the rest of my body!!

I had a wheelchair for first time outside....this was painful! I should have just said when they arrived to get me, but I assumed they were only doing what they'd been told, and that I should be able to sit in a wheelchair by now. They tried to get me to "shift across to chair" in the ambulance... absolutely no chance...do they know what's broken?!

Whilst they went to get someone else for transportation, I sat outside in the air.

Another thing we take for granted. Air.

I haven't been outside of my own accord in weeks.

In fact, I can't go anywhere of my own accord. Another thing we take for granted all too often.

So I sat outside for 20 minutes. Anna actually spotted me whilst she was working. She came and chatted to me briefly before going to get another patient.

And then I was off.

When I arrived at the Winfield, and into room 16, someone actually came and unpacked for me. What on earth?! I don't even get this at home!

My clothes were hung in the wardrobe, toiletries in my ensuite (yes – ensuite) bathroom, and books etc on the table so I could reach them. Not that I've got much stuff....1 Sainsbury's bag and a few bits! That's all I have to show for 14 days in hospital. I think I was still so stubborn and thinking that I would be home in a few days, that I didn't ask for anything else.

To be honest, there's no point in lots of stuff. I'm in bed all day, except for my 10hour trips to the toilet. I've actually started drinking less as it hurts to get off the bed to go the the bathroom.

I must sort that out and drink more....

Don't get me wrong, it's still at the 2 litres a day mark...don't forget, there's not much else to do in hospital...drink, eat, sleep, toilet, drink, eat, sleep etc

Anyway, almost as soon as I arrived, the lady was round to ask what I'd like for my dinner...special was sausage and mash, it would be rude not to! I have a funny feeling the food will be good here. Private and all that.

Now - just to clarify. The main reason I've swapped to private is purely the fact that I can. And mainly the fact that someone else can have my bed in the NHS.

Don't get me wrong - when I was on the ward in Southmead for the first day...I couldn't wait to get out of there. I'd have paid money. But things have improved so much that I actually don't mind where I am. I'm just focusing on recovering.

The other thing about private is that I'll get one on one physio care, worth it's weight in gold when you have such a long journey ahead of you. And given that I'm now officially handed over to the physio's it makes sense to be here.

But, I have to say that the care has been amazing in the NHS - much respect to all those that have treated me, and those that work here.

And the biggest thank you ever!

Ellen came to visit today – so nice to see someone local again. Ellen and Jason have been amazing and stayed in touch throughout. Ellen actually sold me mine and Izzy's house. She showed us around on the 2nd visit and we got talking. Turns out she's from near where I used to live, is divorced, and has 2 girls at the school that Iz is going to in September.

We just hit it off and soon went for wine together.

I digress, later in the day I had my visit from the legend that is Mr Curwen. It's only the 2nd time I've seen him and I feel like I've known him for years. He must be in his 70's and still working full time as an orthopaedic consultant – both private and NHS. And the swearing is still with him! I thought I was bad, but this man is a new level! Must introduce him to my mum....

My first evening here was very relaxed, considering I'm in hospital. There's not a lot else I can do except for relax. I'm horizontal in a bed - albeit a bed that does all sorts of things!!

27th July 2018 - Back to work...sort of!

I actually had a meeting this morning. One of my clients was visiting me in hospital to pull some forms together.

Best get showered and dressed.

Yes, shower...for the first time. Because I've got an ensuite they let me do it. And I was too stubborn to let someone help me. So the nurse sat outside and talked to me instead.

Washed my own hair for the first time.

Washed myself for the first time.

Dried myself for the first time.

And put my clothes on - sort of - for the first time! I needed help with my knickers!! Pesky pelvis and its breaks getting in the way!

So, the client visit was good. I think we covered everything, and I actually felt ok. Shattered by the end of it. But at least I managed the hour.

I actually think I'll end up being friends with all my clients. I spend so much time with them, or talking to them, through a pretty hideous time, that it's hard not to.

Mum and Iz came in to visit. Iz found a new toy to play with in my electric bed...how high could she rise us!! I thought it was great fun, the nurse in charge less so! Admittedly at that point, we were nearly up to the ceiling...can't imagine why she thought it was a safety hazard...

Iz got upset as she was told off for playing with it! Whoops!

Anyway, the done thing is now to bring lunch in with Grandma before heading off to preschool for the afternoon, and then to Daddy's. Loved spending time with Iz, and I feel more human in myself!

Again, I feel the need to context - "feeling more human" - still on 40+ tablets per day. I still can't do a great deal - but I can shower!

Still in bed most of the day.

Still on an old person frame (my interpretation).

Yes, I realise we haven't actually mentioned that..just a piccie earlier. I actually don't care.

It's getting me on my feet. I've already decided that I'm going to try and tick the box of everything my Granny used - in her 90's...and I'm in my 40's!

So, here we go:

Sippy cup - tick

Bib - tick

Zimmer frame - tick

Nappy - no tick

Pads in bed - tick (not mentioned - for a reason!)

Bed with moving mattress to avoid sores - tick (not mentioned either!)

Chair with elevated base - tick

Wheelchair - tick

Commode - OMG! - Tick

Mountain seat for toilet - tick (we'll talk about that!)

So, the mountain seat...it's only actually just become an issue that I realise I have. A normal toilet is actually quite low really, and when you have broken bones everywhere, a complete pain (literally) to get down to.

So, a raised seat (or mountain seat as Iz and I have now labelled it) it is. So much easier. We should all have these, although I suspect it comes under the "lazy" bracket for those that don't actually need them! And it's pretty horrible when you see one on the toilet that you're about to sit on...I always have the thought of "is it clean?".

And then there's the commode....I've only just put it in here as using one has scarred me for life!

Because I have now been told not to weight bear for a couple of days (confusion central with the physio vs the consultant), I can't get to the bathroom properly....so I have to go to the toilet on a commode....by my bed.

Just when I thought things could get no worse!! There is nothing more mortifying that having to press a button to call a nurse, request a commode, and then call them back again to take the wee and poo filled bowl away. Sorry to be graphic, but that's the reality of the situation!

Mind you, poo is incredibly rare these days - try the cocktail of drugs if you ever want to experience constipation to the max!

28th July 2018 - no wine

Physio with Mary. She's the boss, and totally amazing.

When Mary arrived to start my physio, I realised I must be bad. Not everyone gets the boss.

OK, so I'd better take this seriously and put my all into it.

I got a whole raft of new toys..a ball - under inflated, that goes between my knees and I squeeze. A dog walker as I call it - actually called a "leg lifter", and it's used to move your leg that has no strength or feeling in it...so that I can get off the bed etc. Tongs to pick things up - you know, the things that litter pickers have! And, best of all, a plastic sheet to move my legs on with no effort (you can actually use a plastic carrier bag for this!).

Victoria came to visit.

Where's the damn wine?!

I don't think I've ever seen V, aside from in the office, and not had wine, or champagne. More often than not champagne!

Seriously, I'm shocked that she's turned up with no wine. Not that I'm an alcoholic or anything. But it's been over 2 weeks with no alcohol now. A long time for me!

And they did say that I could have some whilst I'm in here…..

Note to self - get Neil on the case!

Anne Marie came in for the afternoon on her way back from her mum's in Bristol. Fabulous to see her too. She bought me goodies as well. I've been thoroughly spoilt, and I'm getting quite a collection of stuff now. Might be up to 3 bags!

Sam and Katie had made me cards :) Bless them, I miss everyone so much and really want to get out of here and back to my normal self.

My cards are everywhere. I feel honoured to have so many friends.

So, a really nice day and visitors are amazing.

And I didn't have to use the commode in front of anyone - bonus!

29th July 2018 - family

Apparently I'm to have no sex for at least 3 months….is someone having a giraffe?! Jeremy Beadle around the corner?

It's honestly the last thing that I can think about at the moment. Can you even imagine sex with a smashed pelvis? Let alone all of the other breaks!

Eyes watering? Say no more!

I was expecting 2 of my cousins, Charlie and Katy today, but I got my aunt and uncle too – bonus! I saw the car arrive in the car park so I knew they were all there. Super excited.

We actually got me into the wheelchair and we went down to the tea room for an hour. I can't explain the bliss I felt to be away from my room for a bit!

It seriously reminded me even more of my dear gran though. Probably as I remember my aunt pushing my gran in a wheelchair, and here she was pushing me now.

Rez and Tamsin (from work at Mars) came in this afternoon. Great to see them. Tamsin's family live a few miles away, and it's only 45 mins for Rez to get to from his home. I feel completely touched, especially as it's Rez's wedding anniversary and he still comes to see me. And I got chocolates too - they won't last long.

New Maltesers Truffles – AMAZING! You must buy them!!

Again - no-one saw me on the commode!!

30th July 2018 - pills and Iz

Iz and mum came in today. Iz and I played on the bed again, until Tracey told Iz off (again), and she sulked....Iz, not Tracey!

Took pills.

Wrote book.

That's it.

Except for the great news that I can weight bear on my left foot again.

Yay! No more commode!

Back to the mountain seat...marginally better than the commode!

31st July 2018 - another day, another load of pills

Iz came in for lunch before she went to nursery, so we had our usual lunch together and lots of left hand side snuggles.

Unfortunately I still can't touch most of my right side, and that means that Iz most definitely can't snuggle on this side either. She's actually been a superstar with regards to touching me and my injuries. She's so careful and always makes sure to ask before she sits anywhere on the bed or anything.

Poor monkey.

It must be really hard for her seeing her mummy like this. And she must struggle to understand. But I can't really talk to her about it yet.

I think we're doing the best we can by acting completely normal about it all. And my mum and Pete have been amazing about looking after her.

Pete is now having her every weekend, and his 2 nights in the week. My mum is having her the other nights at my house, but doing most of the driving to and from Cirencester nursery, and Pete's house in Ashton Keynes. When he moves to Cheltenham things will be much easier.

I'd be lying if I said I wasn't worried about her spending so much time at Pete's. I'm desperately hoping it can't be used against me at any point, and assume no-one would ever even try that given that this is exceptional circumstances caused by a horrific accident.

You'd be seriously sick to use it, right?

01st August 2018 - a turn for the worse

A new month!

My day was actually ok. The usual of eat, sleep, bathroom, TV, physio, pills.

And repeat.

The nurse asked me if I'd like to do my blood thinner injection myself....urrr...no thanks!

Too many memories of IVF and the relentless injections in the stomach.

Seriously relentless for weeks.

Isabel is an IVF baby...mine and Pete's little (or not so little anymore) miracle. She is from our third round of IVF, and came after 4 miscarriages (between 6 and 13 weeks).

Now that's a whole other story!

Anyway, injections in the stomach again daily - torture.

Gill came to visit again and was there at the same time as my mum and Iz. It was a bit of a shame really as I ended up going for x-rays and all sorts whilst they were here so I didn't get to spend much time with them.

I guess when you're in hospital, or when you visit, that's the risk you take, and you don't have a great deal of choice!

I just feel bad that Gill has driven all the way up to see me, and she gets a quick peck on the cheek and a wave from me in my wheelchair as I head downstairs for yet more tests.

So, it's now later in the day....

Bam - out of nowhere....the pain, oh the pain.

I was in tears. First about my back aching beyond belief, and then my left (good) leg.

So, my back was aching, normal really, but hurting a lot more than it usually does. I went to the bathroom in tears because of this, and then just sat on the edge of my bed crying.

But the thing that really got me was the pain in my leg. It was the nerve pain I've been having for a few days. Except that today is different...it's there and it's not going away again.

The top half of my leg has gone numb too.

It's a violent stabbing kind of pain. I can't really describe it.

I get that my right leg should be suffering, but my left leg?!

That's my good leg and I rely on it! Admittedly my left foot is broken, but to be honest that doesn't even bother me in the grand scheme of things.

As I'm sat in tears, I have nurses and on call doctors all looking very concerned and flocking into my room to see me.

Ice packs galore came out.

More pain killers got put in me.

And Mr Curwen was called. He was at the cinema with his wife...I think he'd been dragged there as they were seeing Mamma Mia 2!

He wasn't concerned and said to monitor me over night - not concerned?! I am!!

The ice packs and pain relief got things under control for the night...as long as I stayed still.

Don't fancy going to the toilet again tonight... would rather wet myself than have that pain again!

This could scupper my plans of going home on Friday so I'm feeling really low about it all. I wanted to be home on Friday for my birthday as I thought that it would make a really nice celebration. And would also mean that I am home for Mum's 70th on Saturday. And I'd be home for my little girl - the most important person to me in the whole world.

Bugger.

2nd August 2018 - live with it

So, the nerve pain might be a permanent feature. It could be as a result of the trauma suffered by my pelvis in the accident and the nerve damage that may have come with it.

Or, it could be just until the 12 week operation to remove the scaffolding around my pelvis.

Let's hope it's this option rather than the former.

Or, it could be the nerve having been trapped in my pelvic operation.

Another one to think about...not sure how that gets remedied so I'll just push aside in my mind for now.

I feel supremely rubbish about it, but I'm not going to let it stop me going home tomorrow.

Sometimes I love my stubbornness, sometimes I hate it!

So, Mary got on the case with my physio again. She is working relentlessly to ensure that I am prepared for home tomorrow. I have to do the stairs today otherwise I won't be allowed home.

To be honest, after the pain last night, I'll be surprised if I'm allowed home at all.

Damn it - I've been asked again about doing the blood thinner injection myself. I guess I had better give it a go, just to check that I'm doing it right... especially given that I'm going to have 6 weeks of it at home!

I found this out today...rats! It literally is like being on IVF again, without the baby to show at the end of it.

6 weeks....42 days....42 needles.

I know people do this all the time (diabetes etc), but I really hate needles...and I'm a total wimp really.

3rd August 2018 – birthday and home

So - big day...

Hmmm – how do I feel about going home? Excited, nervous, unsettled...

Mary asked me specifically "what are you most afraid of about going home?"

Me "my mum, and how she will be. I know she doesn't think I should be going home yet and I'll be thinking about that all the time. She'll blame everything on my being home too early and me doing too much".

And it all played through. I actually hate it when I'm right about something like this. But I also know that it's only because my mum cares so much, love her.

But, before I go home, there's so many people to say goodbye to. This place has been my home for the last 8 nights and I have actually quite enjoyed being here.

I say quite enjoyed...but to context it - I've made the most of my situation. I've spoken to the nurses about them and their lives, I've enjoyed the food, I've been out around the grounds - albeit in a wheelchair, I've spoken to other patients when learning to walk in the corridors, and I've talked to the reception staff whenever I've been past them.

Ok, I know it's not much, but there's a limit to how much you can do with multiple broken bones in a hospital!!

I also thought I'd get myself weighed on the way out.

Over 3 weeks in hospital with NO alcohol and a heck of a lot of trauma to my body. And there was the first week where I barely ate anything! Surely I've lost at least a stone? Maybe 2?

Ur - no.

EXACTLY the same weight as when I last weighed myself, at home, before the accident.

Clearly the scales are broken...and I told the nurse, who was less than convinced!!

My taxi home was actually better than I thought. No grabbing the door handle, no leaping out of the seat, no covering my eyes, no pain in my bones.

I think the driver was quite relieved too!

Let's not mention why I'm getting a taxi…

So, mentally I felt ok, and physically I felt ok. Things were going well so far.

I got home about 13.30.

Iz was there waiting with mum, together with flowers and pressies for my birthday - love them both!

I dumped my 2 Sainsbury's bags from the hospital and sat down in the lounge. I then spent the afternoon "chilling".

I'm not sure my mum feels that relaxed about having me home. She is on edge the whole time, and won't sit down and do nothing.

I'm also not sure how it felt to be "home"…odd if I'm honest. And not like my home really as I can't do anything for myself or for anyone else.

And "home"…the place I completed on 3 weeks before my accident and then spent 2 of those 3 weeks away on holiday.

Anyway, you'll like this one…specific question from my mum…I'd been home approx. 30 minutes

"do you think your accident will change your habits in the car?"

Red rag to a bull.

I WASN'T DOING ANYTHING WRONG.

I don't know why I'm so angry. Probably because I've spent the last 3 weeks in hospital desperate to know what happened on the 12th of July, and knowing that I wasn't doing anything I shouldn't be doing. But 3 weeks of stewing on it and I've convinced myself of all sorts of scenarios. I guess it's natural, but it doesn't feel good, I feel like I'm going mad.

Neil arrived at about 1930 as he was late dropping the boys back from their holiday in Devon. He came laden with flowers, presents, and drinks... love him. Unfortunately I didn't feel like drinking as I was shattered....I definitely will do tomorrow though!

Although Mum "usually" drops Iz at Pete's on a Friday night for the weekend, Iz is staying here tonight so that she can be here for the morning of Mum's birthday.

I say "usually" as it's become a bit of the norm after 4 weeks.

Amazing how quickly things can change in life....

4th August 2018 - Mum and Uncle P turn 70!

Mum was up and about before I got a chance to move! I wished her a happy birthday but she was on the go already. We did all manage to have breakfast in my bed to celebrate though.

Iz tickled Neil's feet where he was sleeping, in her bed, to wake him....!

Pete picked Iz up at 1300 after we'd had cake and pressies for mum.

It wasn't quite the 70th birthday I had planned for my mum, but at least we're all still here to see it.

I had booked a few days away in the Lakes, but obviously I've cancelled it....walking up hills and mountains doesn't seem likely even in the near future, let alone now.

Granny Faye, Auntie Nic, and Jake came over about 1400 on their way back from Devon. It was great to see them all! Poor Jake was bored so we found a film for him whilst we all chilled in the garden.

I found that the outside garden chairs are actually quite comfortable for a broken person ;-) We had a couple of glasses of fizz and wine, together with a lovely afternoon in sunshine with everyone chatting.

Laurence also popped over from opposite. Juliette and the kids are in Germany on their holidays and

Laurence is joining them next week. A couple more beers for the boys and everyone is happy.

Boy, am I paying for it now....I feel shattered and have definitely done too much. And it's only 1800!

5th August 2018 - just chilling

Today I relaxed my bones and injuries with my bottom on the sofa all day...I say my bottom...it's actually my whole body as I can't actually sit for more than 10 minutes yet!

We had a nightmare this evening though as I got stuck in the garden chair (in the lounge). I can't believe the pain I was in. Neil called an ambulance as the pain was horrific and we needed help. I couldn't get out of the chair due to the pain, and the pain needed attention. 2 hours later we were still waiting as I wasn't an emergency (understandably). I needed the toilet desperately so I had the choice of getting up through the pain or peeing myself...I managed to get up. The last thing I wanted was to go back to hospital too.

So Neil called the ambulance off...phew.

I've promised him I'm ok.

I'm sleeping on the sofa too as my room has been prepped for it's new furniture, and I'm more comfortable not moving at the moment.

6th August 2018 – Hanging clothes again...or not!

Nicholas arrived at 0830 from the wardrobe company to fit my new wardrobes...yay!

I'm going to be able to put my clothes away and go to sleep in my own bed tonight!

Amazing, I can't wait!

Ok, so things didn't quite go to plan....Nicholas doesn't have all the parts....not even enough parts so that what he's put together is suitable for hanging space.

Nightmare.

But at least he's had a mail by the time he leaves to say that it will all be sorted by Friday 10th August.

Phew – not too long to go without my bed, or my new wardrobes.

Sofa again for me tonight....it's not like I've got broken bones or anything....only 24 of them...

7th August 2018 - bad day

The police came around today and I got my phone back at last. I felt incredibly nervous for some reason.

When PC Stephen Drewitt arrived, I was surprised that there were 2 of them that came in. This made me feel even more nervous! But Neil was there with me so that helped.

When we finally got into my phone (I couldn't remember the PIN as it was brand new the day before my accident), they spent what felt like an eternity going through it.

All clear.

As I said right from the start.

Absolutely no calls/texts/emails from the accident.

For some reason they thought it odd that I was so nervous...urrr....because they made me wait nearly 4 weeks!! What did they expect!?!

Anyway – phone, make up (critical!), and watch back.

I was happy.

Until the police decided to put me under caution for a statement.

I felt very uncomfortable being under caution, but more than happy to give a statement as I'm very strongly of the opinion that a horrible accident has happened.

Nothing more, nothing less.

And I don't actually remember anything so there's not actually anything to say.

Long and short of it though - I understand that the initial collision report may show that the point of impact was on the other side of road...this would therefore mean it could be my fault.

Other causes? Speed? Road conditions? Driver avoidance?

None of which have been considered yet, and I have to wait for up to 6 months to find out more.

I felt horrific, and I asked both Neil and my mum to leave.

All I could do was to look at all my flowers and cards and think "I don't deserve these", "I don't deserve any help from anyone".

This isn't me being negative. It's my emotions. It's how I felt.

I can honestly say I have never felt so horrendous in my entire life. I can only explain it as something has happened that I have no recollection of, and I'm potentially going to be blamed for the fall out from it. In particular the injuries that someone else is also suffering from.

Mum refused to leave and came into the lounge eventually. She was so upset. We both cried together.

On the positive side, I've got my TAG watch back that I've had for years and thought had been lost in the accident. That and my makeup bag :)

There are good things in life, and I could be worse off. There are plenty of others that are in a worse position than me, and I will always remember that.

So, I feel rubbish now, but I will drag myself out of it as I know that I'm phenomenally lucky - both to be here, but also to be in the position that I'm in in life.

8th August 2018 - still low

For some reason I'm particularly cheesed off today that none of my old family (aside from my ex mum in law, who has been lovely and called my mum to check how things are etc) have been in touch to see how I am.

I sent them all a mail on the 28th July to update them on my condition and didn't receive any replies. I literally wrote everything in my mail - the extent of my injuries, the fact that I nearly died, thanking them for all looking after Iz etc. I am truly grateful for everyone pulling together and giving Iz the love and care she needs whilst I'm in this mess.

I asked Pete about my accident as I can only think that he didn't realise the extent of it all, and therefore others haven't either.

Thankfully the police called him on the day of my accident and explained the accident but that I would be ok in the long run.

Everyone handles things differently and I guess I can't expect people to be the same as me.

My accident has, more than anything previously, highlighted to me that life is too short to hold grudges from things that have happened in the past.

No matter how big or small.

If you are connected then find a way to make things work, for both yourself and others.

9th August 2018 - drugs

The pain...the pain...the pain....god it's boring! I must take my drugs...note to self!

It's only been 4 weeks.

I've realised that if I don't keep up with painkillers then my back and leg kill me. I can't get comfortable in any position!

I'm not saying anymore, I'm just taking tablets and sleeping.

10th August 2018 - more drugs

When I finally leapt (ha ha - just to see if you're reading this!!) out of bed I had to get dressed and look presentable.

Suzi came to visit us today.

Suzi is Izzy's second mummy as she looked after her for 3 years+ from 10months to over 4 years old. She is a mummy now too, so came to visit us with baby Jax. He's too cute.

It's nice to have a visitor, I'm just still not in the "home" mode. And I hate needing help for everything.

Literally everything.

I even have to pee with the door open as I can't always get down or up from the mountain seat.

Once I climbed back into bed later on today, I thought about the fact that I'm so sick of sleeping on my back. All I want to do is curl up on my side, cuddle Neil, reach across the bed for the light....whatever...just not lie still on my bloody back!

Randomly, I also have this constant worry that something internal will go wrong....I have to keep taking the tablets.

My worry is from all the internal injuries that I suffered. We've not really spoken about them and the severity of them at the time. I had internal bleeding from my liver and spleen. It doesn't sound too good to me, but apparently they heal themselves.

My carotid artery heals itself too - I had no idea that so many people actually die if they rupture this, as I did...good job I'm still here.

It still doesn't stop me worrying that something internal is going to go wrong.

I'm cold today...is that a sign of something?

This is the extent of my paranoia at the moment. I hope it improves!

11th August 2018 - Heat is the way forward

Today I stayed in bed until 1030 – bliss. Bed is actually the most comfortable place at the moment, even if I am having to lie on my back, with a pillow under my knees. And the pillow barricade down the middle...so that Iz doesn't kick me when she's in my bed!

And it's still cold. I have my duvet back on.

Fiona (Mum's friend from Chipping Norton) has sent me a drawing and painting kit...what a lovely lady. I'm going to send her a thank you card tomorrow.

Mum went out into town at lunchtime – she desperately needs a break – I'm going to book her a spa treatment for next week to give her some time to herself.

Neil came over with his dad and the boys. We were going to go for lunch at the café around the corner, but they closed at lunchtime, so they ended up going home and I had hummus and breadsticks under the blanket in the lounge!

Mum and I watched Casualty tonight – car crash... marvellous. So factually incorrect, it's brilliant.

Bless my mum...halfway through the episode she asked if I was ok to watch it!

To be honest, I've been glued to helicopter rescue programmes since my accident. Is that weird? I went in one after all...

Seeing an ambulance is different though. Not sure why. It's not even as though I went in one from the actual accident.

12th August 2018 - 31 days

So...a month to the day...as I wake in bed I think nothing has changed...

Oh yes, it has!

I can't move without searing pain,
And my legs don't work,
And I can't get out of bed without crutches.
And I can't wee without a granny seat on the toilet (this one's funny!).
I can't carry anything as I'm using these damn

crutches the whole time.

I need a live in helper (my poor mum).

I do nothing all day, except for write this book...that I hope will raise thousands for charity.

And worst of all, my little girl isn't here, and it's my weekend with her. But her daddy is looking after her on weekends until I'm better.

But...I'll get better. Some people never do. So I count my lucky stars today, and every day since 12th July 2018.

I WILL get better x

So – that was whilst lying in bed....suddenly I realise it's 0900 and Iz is back at 1000 from her daddy's....best move my sorry backside out of bed then!

So – today I managed to put my knickers on for the first time on my own!!

Yay – MAJOR triumph....minor I hear you say...
MAJOR I say back to you!!

I managed to have a wash on my own, I managed to fully dress on my own, AND I managed to wash my hair on my own. It's a bloody miracle....all the things we take for granted normally...and I'm now struggling to do them on my own. It's a sad state of affairs.

BUT, I'm on the mend!

Iz got back bang on 1000! Pete couldn't get out the house quick enough – he must be shattered, he's trying to hold down a job too.

Katy, Neil, Megan and Tom arrived at 1100 – it was so nice to see them! Iz and I were actually meant to see them the weekend after my accident so it's really nice to have them all. I mentioned Katy at the start of the book...we FaceTimed on the night of my accident, not that I really remember it.

Anyway, they were superstars and bought loads of snacky foods for lunch with them. The kids were amazing and played together in the basement (it's a playroom...not as bad as it sounds!), so much so that Iz was gutted when they left – she adores Megan and Tom.

Neil (my Neil) picked us up as Katy and Neil left, and we went to his for the afternoon. I can't say I was relishing the idea of spending the afternoon with 4 more kids...what possessed me??!!

Ok, so there were 4 adults too, but 5 kids in total?! 4 of which were boys!! Mad I hear you say.... you chose to do that?!

Your choice...blah blah... I know, I'm insane...blame the drugs!

The lovely Granny Faye (Neil's mum) cooked us all a roast so it was actually lovely - and there were loads of roast potatoes, always a bonus!

But, surprise surprise, I've done too much for the day.

I'm also concerned as my left side is hurting...it's been like it for a few days around my lower rib cage.

Mum thinks it's because I've been doing too much, but as I said, that's only today, and not the last 4 days.

I called the hospital as when I looked at Dr Google (font of all knowledge to the 21st centurions...) it suggested that the spleen is in that area. My main concern now was that I lacerated my spleen in the accident, and now that area was hurting inside me.

Interestingly I haven't looked at Google throughout my whole time since my accident, this was the first time in weeks. To be honest, I haven't actually been interested and I've purely listened to the experts...the way we used to work before we had the internet!

Anyway, I got a taxi to Gloucester A&E as Cheltenham was closing for the night. I had to leave mum at home as Iz was sleeping blissfully in bed (my bed!), and Neil was sorting the boys out at his house.

A&E were brilliant, once they figured out that I couldn't sit for long periods of time and that I'd had a significant accident recently. Admittedly it took Neil telling them when he got there, and me crying in pain - not just my giving them the list of injuries at the start and them seeing my records. They swiftly got me onto a flat bed in the trauma unit.

Hopefully I'd be done quickly.

Canular in, wrist band on...I started fearing the worst.

That I'd be admitted .... AGAIN.

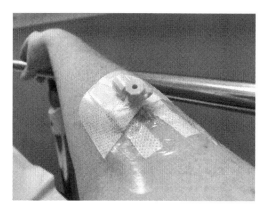

Neil took a spin in the wheelchair to entertain himself!

After 4 hours, 2 nurses, 1 doctor, 1 surgeon, more bloods, and a lot of prodding...I'm on my way home again, with more broken bones...3 more ribs.

Pah – what's another 3 broken ribs on top of everything else!?!

At least it's not my spleen.....every cloud and all that...

27 bones now, not that I'm counting or anything.

Did you know that the human body has 206 bones (for an average adult)?

So I've broken way over 10% of my bones. That's impressive....even by my standards!

Simple things impress me these days!

13th August - boredom

So today I thought I'd stay in bed all day to try and give my ribs a bit of a chance to stop hurting.

This lasted until 1030, when I got bored and got up!!

Oh - I haven't mentioned that my wardrobes didn't get finished on the 10th August as promised. And now I'm having a battle with the company providing them as I'm having to sleep on a sofa more often than not with all my broken parts. Ludicrous.

At least it gives me something to do.

14th August - much more productive

Gill came today, and was a total superstar...
She bought food and flowers, and did loads round the house for me and with me. Cooking, tidying up, making beds. It's things that I have wanted to do but needed help to do them. But I feel really guilty asking my mum. She's so tired - obviously -

and I hate to think of myself adding to that. I know I can't help what happened and the way I am now, but it doesn't stop the guilt.

I've sent my mum to have her feet done this afternoon - she loves having them done and she needs some polish on desperately! I actually want to force her to have a break as she won't sit down at all at home and sending her out seems to be the only option!

My mum finds things to do even when there really is nothing that needs doing. Today she found some washing to put on in a bag of clothes I was taking for my cousin at the weekend - it was all clean already and didn't need washing again!

"The Pain" in my left leg is back. I've not really mentioned it for a while. Simply because I've actually found a way to get rid of it when it comes on. I move straight away and find another position to sit in - i.e move my bum cheek!

I was trying to moisturise my feet as I was so chuffed that I could reach them for the first time since before 12th July...premature again!! I can't actually reach them without significant pain!

Stubbornness...it's not always good for us.

15th August - Physio

In the words of "Peter and Jane":
FML....physiotherapy today. Painful is the only way to describe it.

This was my first session since leaving the hospital a couple of weeks ago. They wanted to give my body a break and to let me get used to being home again which is understandable.

Although painful, Fiona was so knowledgeable. I learnt loads about my injuries and how the body works to heal over time. I also had a reality check (which I get quite a lot of) on how long it will take to recover to a reasonable level.

Just to remind myself when I read this back - at least a year, and some injuries will always cause me issues.

It was weird going back to The Winfield Hospital. It was my home for over a week, and I felt safe there. The nurses became my extended family. And although I was only there a for few days in the grand scheme of things, it felt like longer, and it still felt odd to go back there as an out-patient.

Maybe I could stay in the waiting room and sleep there....! The food was pretty good too!

It's also hard to think that things just continue on. A new set of patients come in, and then go. New operations, new physiotherapy patients etc.

As a great result today, I got my possessions back from my car. Neil was an absolute star and collected them for me. I couldn't have gone to the place where it was, although I now know that my car was destroyed on 23rd July so wasn't even there to see anymore. It would have still felt too weird though and I'm glad I wasn't there.

The bag of belongings even smelt of old cars, if that makes any sense.

I don't know why I thought there were so many great things in my car...but I did get my Hunter Wellies back!

16th August – Big Day….6 hours off sofa, and surgeons

So today I got taken down to Southmead Hospital in Bristol, to the fracture clinic. I actually thought this appointment was some kind of sick joke. They posted it to me a couple of weeks ago so that I received it just after returning from my stint in hospital. I had to phone them to confirm that it was serious as I couldn't see how on earth I was meant to get to an appointment in Bristol so soon after my accident. I couldn't even stand up, let alone travel.

I actually got taken in a service offered by the NHS. A lovely man called Chris picked me up from my house and drove me there, door to door, for free. And he's a volunteer. Amazing service, thank you yet again to our NHS.

People in the waiting room were comparing injuries...I was dreading my turn....um...take your pick!

Still I felt in a much better position than most though. The only explanation that I have for this is my mental attitude towards the situation.

I could have died.

I'm still here.

I have my health and all my limbs.

I have my family and friends.

And I have a home to live in.

I'm exceptionally lucky and I'm very clear on that. I've always felt that though, it's not just as a result of my accident, although it could easily be the case.

My X-rays took a phenomenally long time as there were so many to do. It's laughable really. I'm sure the guy was chuckling with me. He talked me through all the pictures and explained where the new bone was growing in all the different areas etc...I can't believe the knowledge of these guys, it's incredible and made me feel incredibly humble.

I managed to walk some of the way on my crutches - hooray.

And I managed to see Mr Mez Acharya – the main man. The wonderful man who operated on me for the whole day on Saturday 14th July 2018. I gave him the biggest hug I think I've ever given anyone. I'm so grateful to him and his team for putting my bones back in the right place...sort off. Or plates across them where they couldn't put them back together! To be honest, my insides look like a building site and I'm full of metal.

I can't wait to go through customs....

So, Mr Acharya was amazing and took pictures of all of my X-rays for me so I can add them in here:

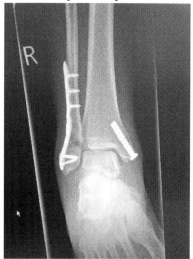

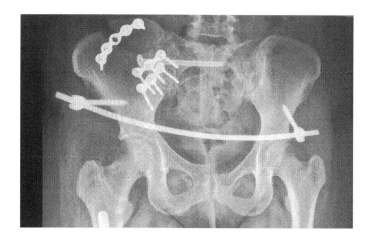

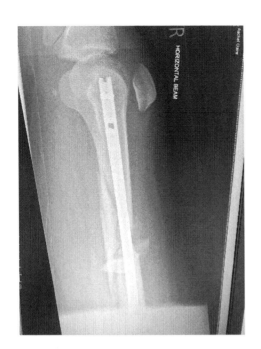

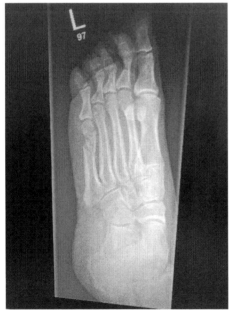

He wants a copy of this book, so here you go Mr Acharya – I'll make sure one is on your desk - you are amazing and I'll always remember what you've done for me, thank you!

As a complete aside, on the off chance I put a video of Iz on Facebook tonight. She's desperate to get in touch with her first ever love, Lewis, from Crete back in June - before any of this happened. They only actually spoke on the last day (after making eyes, in a 4 or 5 year old kind of way, all week), but he kissed her (on the cheek!!) and she's besotted! She's 4, he's 5. Love it!

I've absolutely no idea how I'm going to find him given that there are 60m of us living in the UK, and he is a mere 1 of us.

Hey Ho! I've put the video on so we'll see what the power of social media does.

Friday 17th August - First night out - woo hoo

My daytime was the same as usual...the plans to do nothing all day did not materialise as I'm too fidgety and stubborn.

I got up 0830, washed, sorted Iz out with a bath together with Grandma's help. I got her dressed (Iz..not Grandma!). I washed my hair. I got dressed. I sorted my room (as much as a complete cripple does!!).

And I managed to make it downstairs for…wait for it….1030!

Mum and Iz headed to the park on Iz's new scooter that I have bought for her….iScoot Blaze. I'm not sure I'll be going on one anytime soon….

She didn't realise it had flashing wheels until she scooted off!!

I spent an hour or so sorting nothing, and then they were back.

I had lunch with Iz and then we had chill time….Finding Dory…. AGAIN!

Pete picked Iz up at 1530 and I struggled to be too friendly as I can't get my head around the way my accident is being handled by some people. He's an amazing daddy, but my morals are being called into question by trying to be friends with someone who thinks completely differently to me.

I guess it's a way of handling things. To think that I'm fine from my accident may be the easiest thing to do and the best way for some to handle it. I guess it's what I'm doing to an extent too.

"Fine" = "Excellent in character or ability"

I'm seriously not "fine".

Anyway, onto better things.

Neil and I went out tonight. This was the first time for me in 5 weeks! Woo hoo! It's a miracle!

Our taxi arrived at 1845 and was somewhat challenging for me to get into.

We got to the Giggling Squid in town and had a 3 course meal, wine, and beer for 2 of us. All of this for £15 – thanks to their lovely head office who sent me a voucher due to my accident – thank you!

A truly amazing meal – you have to go there if you're in Cheltenham at all.

The most significant bit of the night for me though....I need the toilet....

Hmmm – stairs.

Ok – disabled toilet.

Now, don't get me wrong, I've used a disabled loo plenty of times. When I've been drunk and no one else has been queueing for it in a pub or club.

Never sober, or because I've actually needed to like I have in the last few weeks.

It felt different. Very different. And I have to say, not in a good way. I'm not sure why, it just hit me.

Anyway, we had a good night out, and that's the main thing.

Saturday 18th August - New wheels and wine!

Let's hope I can drive again soon as the Audi A5 here is mine from the end of the month!

Neil and I popped in to see some friends and we also went to have wine with Ellen and Jason down the road. They've just been in the Lombok earthquake so it was fascinating to hear all about that…and scary too.

They are both all in one piece though so that's good.

We headed of to Hertfordshire about 1745 to see Chris and Charlie, and baby Maisie. Baby Maisie who so isn't a baby anymore, it's just that Iz and I have always called her that!

We had a curry with Chris as Charlie was at the cinema with Kim and Sarah (her mum and sister in law), and then went to bed at 2300ish to get some sleep before chaos descends tomorrow.

Sunday 19th August – Shower and PARTY!!

Or not….it's hard to party on crutches! But I had lovely cuddles with Baby Henry.

Oh, and I had a decent shower at Charlie's as they have a walk in one. Fab! I felt so clean I squeaked! Not literally!

It was really good to see all the family too, some of whom I haven't seen since way before the accident, and the rest since I was in hospital. Everyone was amazed that I had made it over.

As I've said before, I will not let this beat me.

And I will continue to be stubborn!

On the way home we stopped off in Chieveley to see Neil's Uncle and Aunt. It was great to see them too.

Uncle Fred had a great idea to get in touch with the Scottish TV channel re Lewis (little boy from Crete) and Iz.

So I did.

Now, I still don't actually know if it was the TV activity or social media, but within 30 minutes I had friend request from Tommy. I actually thought he was a weirdo initially, but it's Lewis's dad!!

I've found him!

Iz is going to be so excited. I can't wait to tell her when she gets back from Pete's tomorrow!

Anyway, when we get home I want to do some bits....and there's nothing worse than wanting to move things around and not being able to as you have no spare hands.

I want to move some vases of flowers in the lounge, but I can't as I need to use the crutches in my hands to move everywhere. I don't feel like I can ask Neil as he's shattered and he's driven everywhere all weekend. And I definitely won't feel like I can ask mum tomorrow as she'll be too tired with doing everything else.

Oh well, not the biggest trauma, it's just incredibly frustrating!

Actually I feel like a complete burden. Neil is shattered and not in the mood at all to help me with things around the house. Mum is back tomorrow and she will be shattered looking after Iz.

I'm going to bed....shattered too, but more mentally than physically I think.

Monday 20th August - will I ever be able to sneeze properly again?

And my gorgeous godson, Sam's, birthday – I can't believe he's 11 today!

Happy Birthday Sam!

So 4 sneezes in bed....well, I can't really call them sneezes! I'm actually too scared that my pelvis will explode if i do a proper sneeze.

And it hurts.

8 sneezes in a row is apparently the equivalent of an orgasm....guess I won't be doing that for a long time either!!

I'm on a mission today.

As I said last night, I want to move 2 vases of flowers in the lounge but hate asking for help all the time.

So I did it myself.

Both moved successfully around my lounge! I held onto the poof for some stability, and it was seriously hard work.

So trivial. But so incredibly rewarding.

Also, I'm sick of crawling up the last 3 stairs in my house so I've found a way to use my crutches on them. I'm sure that my Physio/Health&Safety

would have something to say about the method, but it's liberating...

My goodness, who'd have thought I'd say that a few months ago!

On the plus side, I can now actually get up the stairs without sticking my arse in the air and crawling the last 3 steps. It wasn't me at my best!

Iz is back. Daddy and I were on good terms which was nice.

I've just told Iz that we've found Lewis, and she wants to see him...now...groan!

I've shown her some pictures of him to try and pacify her for the time being. He lives in Scotland, in case that wasn't apparent! And now she's even gone all shy about it when we try to do a video for him - love her! I'm sure I was much older when I got like this!

She's downstairs with Grandma now as I'm trying to have some sleep in bed. Jess the cat has joined me under the duvet as it's the only place to get some relief from little people.

Tuesday 21st August - horrible burden

I'm feeling like a burden.

Again.

I feel like I shouldn't be asking for anything at all, and even a pint of water feels cheeky.

Everyone seems tired. Whether it's tired of me asking or not is another matter! Specifically Neil and Mum, who do everything for me at the moment bless them.

It's the worst feeling. Worse than my accident itself. Especially when you've been so independent for as long as I have.

I have literally needed nothing for years and years. I do everything for myself.

And now I can do nothing. I need help for everything.

So humbling.

Anyway...enough of that sympathy spiel.

After being kicked by the octopus (Iz) in the night numerous times, I was awake early anyway this morning. Iz was stirring from 0600, and when she woke properly at 0700 she was surprised to find me wide awake.

Funny that.

I felt productive when I finally got out of bed. When I say "got out of bed" it sounds so simple... what I actually mean is:

Move my legs, which feel like dead weights, around to the side of the bed in slow motion.

Deal with the nerve pain that hits me almost every time I move my left leg anywhere to the side.

Sit up (Ha! That's a joke in itself!).

Take deep breaths and gain some strength.

And stand, like Bambi, whilst getting my balance (and crutches).

Oh, and all of this has to be at least 20 minutes after I've taken the morning's quota of drugs – only 10 in the morning now!

I've actually totalled up the number of tablets I now take in a day.

Drum roll please.......32. Oh, plus 1 injection in my stomach each evening.

The injection has got to be my favourite (not!) – prodding my stomach every evening like a pin cushion.

Which bit of my stomach will be most receptive this evening?

Urrrr – none!

Pick a bit of flab...any bit of flab...!

Actually, my stomach looks like a tie-dye now.

Remember those from school?

Here's a picture for you if not, and if you do remember them then you'll appreciate the picture too.

Anyway – back to this morning.

I actually put some clothes away in my new drawers in my room. So simple, yet so satisfying.

I put my new mirror up on the wall (with the help of mum), and sorted through my other clothes before the wardrobe company return AGAIN to do more to my wardrobes on Thursday. I say "more" because they apparently still won't finish. I can't even type about it properly as I'm so angry with them.

I've even told them that they are mentioned in this book...not in a particularly good light.

I've actually got friends that have used them and got amazing furniture, but my experience has been awful. It's such a shame as the wardrobes will actually be lovely, if they are ever finished.

After I finished in my room, I bought myself a wheelchair.

Yep - a wheelchair!

Things I never thought I'd do. At least not until I was a significant number of years older than 42 anyway. But I'm not going to stay inside and become a total hermit for the next few months so this my way of getting out and about.

I've discovered that wheelchairs can be as cheap or as expensive as you like and want to spend. I've stuck to the cheaper end as I really don't plan on using it for too long.

Not sure how long my body is planning on using one for....

I'm in bed by 2130 – it's rock n roll in my life these days.

(Not that it was even before my accident!)

And I'll have to set my alarm for 2330 to take my tablets as there's absolutely no way I can stay awake until then, and I definitely can't survive the night without them.

Wednesday 22nd August - exercise

I've discovered a new way of taking my tablets – take them in the night when I wake up naturally needing them, and not actually set an alarm for somewhere around 2300.

A much better option. I can hear you asking why I've not done this before and I've absolutely no idea!

Anyway, I woke up after 0800 with a start and flew out of bed.

Flew in the sense that I threw the duvet off, and crawled as fast as I could with a shattered pelvis, leg, and 2 broken feet...

See, I thought that the wardrobe man was due today at 0800.

Nope.

It's tomorrow.

I realised as soon as I was upright.

So I sank back into bed and mum brought me breakfast up – bless her.

I wonder if Neil will do the same tomorrow...

When I finally got up and dressed, Jason came over to measure up for my extension/conversion. I'm not letting my accident stop me doing the things I want to do. It may delay them slightly, but I won't let it stop them.

I just need to figure out what I can afford now that my money is being spent somewhat differently to my original plan, and on top of this I'm not earning anything.

Neil arrived at lunchtime so that we could go and try out the Hilton DoubleTree swimming pool.

Arrived.

Stairs to go anywhere you needed.

Great.

I go to the reception desk and ask "where's the access for disabled people please?". The receptionist threw her hand in the distance somewhere and said just along the side of the building. So we wandered along the side (as much as you can on crutches) and found ourselves at the leisure centre....more stairs to descend than ever. Oh well, I may as well just climb down them and get it over with rather than returning to the receptionist to find another way.

We got passes and a free towel each (saved a whopping 50p) and went to get changed.

Again, no idea how you're meant to do this as a heterosexual couple where one is essentially crippled.

There are male changing rooms, and female changing rooms. That's it.

No disabled ones. No options for a couple where one needs to help the other.

OK - I can do this....and I did. I did already have my swimsuit on to be fair.

I got in the pool in no time at all. I actually think Neil was more nervous than me as he seemed very twitchy.

Actually, putting my crutches down by the pool steps and getting in was really easy.

As long as no-one else minds my crutches being lobbed out on the side for them all to trip over then we're ok!

Being in the water was a really weird feeling.

As in no feeling. I could move around in any way I wanted with no pain to be felt at all.

I still couldn't walk though. It wasn't for want of me trying, I just couldn't get my right leg to work. I couldn't get it to step in front of my left leg. Or anywhere to be honest.

I must ask Fiona on Friday about this.

When we got out of the pool, Neil asked me how I found it. "Yeah, no problem, better than I thought".

A couple of hours later and I can barely move. My pelvis has locked up and my knee is screaming at me.

The most comedy moment of all was when I tried to get myself up the stairs to get changed. I probably looked like the drunkest person on the planet as I literally crawled up them (and yes I did have my arse in the air!).

Pain aside, I'm so sick of looking at the four walls of my living room that I fancy going out again tonight.

So, for the second time in a week, Neil and I headed out. The Wine Bar in Charlton Kings this time and 2 very large glasses of red for me please! Not at the same time, obviously.

What I didn't count on was the pain in my tummy that suddenly hit me whilst we were out.

Ok, one for the ladies...Now I know that we constantly think about our jeans being too tight right?

So, now I have to think about my jeans rubbing where my blood thinner injection has gone in this evening ASWELL as them being too tight generally.

Seriously, I had to undo my jeans in a public place as it was stinging so much!

A whole new thought to jeans....at least I can get into them again though. This is a first since the accident. Too many cuts and bruises for them to be comfortable before now.

We had dinner at The Looking Glass, a new restaurant in Charlton Kings. It's not in "the village" though so I'm not sure how many locals have actually tried it.

Food brilliant, service excellent.

Home for some bubbles after this and a write up of the first week after my accident which is understandably a little foggy on the brain.

And we're definitely going to need those bubbles for it.

Back to week 1 for us, but not for you as you will have read it already earlier on in here.

Thursday 23rd August - wardrobes I can actually use!

I'm out of bed early for a change and my bedroom is set for finishing (except for 1 door) the wardrobes.

Nick arrives at 0825 and gets straight to work. I feel bad as I don't actually make him anything to drink until 1300. I had absolutely no strength today. I think the swimming yesterday took it out of me. I slept on the sofa until just before 1300, hence the lack of drinks.

I guess it could also have something to do with the bubbles we drank last night....

Hmmmm.....

Ok, so the amazing story of Lewis and Iz (cast your minds back to the Scottish boy that she met on her holidays and that we found on Facebook) is not going to be shared anymore for personal reasons.

I can't believe that so many TV channels etc are interested in that story, but not in the near death car accident of 2 people who go on to survive.

Obviously the press don't do stories that are just about raising awareness and money for charity.

It's actually pretty unbelievable and goes to show that the press purely focus on trash.

Or maybe it's just the press that I'm reading that does this!?!

My knee has just stopped stinging now. Bonus.

I haven't really mentioned this, but it's been going on for a few days and it was starting to concern me. I think it must have been part of the healing process where things are gradually coming back to life. Either that or the forest of hairs on it as it needs shaving desperately!

Now, that's another subject that we've not really touched on either...and you certainly wouldn't have wanted to touch on my legs in the last few weeks. They are horrendous.

And when I say horrendous, I mean HORRENDOUS.

I was mortified when the nurse at The Winfield took the plaster off my right leg after the first 3 weeks. It was like a jungle on that leg.

See, I have managed to get both my mum and Neil to shave my legs as much as possible so far, but it's not the same as doing it myself. And I still can't go anywhere near the wounds on both legs and feet.

So - showering, shaving, hair washing...all things that I just did before, without a second thought, are all pretty traumatic now.

And they definitely bring a new meaning to the term 'hard work'.

Surely I must be burning some extra calories somewhere?! The weight must be dropping off right?!

Anyway - I'm hoping for another shower either tomorrow (if I can convince mum and Iz to come swimming with me), or Saturday when I'm definitely swimming as I'm having my feet done at the hotel too.

My feet are disgusting.

Imagine your feet being packed away in a bag for weeks, and all the skin that would accumulate.

That's my feet!

Again, mortified.

Interestingly my toe nails don't appear to have grown since before my accident. I have realised that my body is sending all of its energy to all the places that need to heal, rather than to other areas such as my nails and hair.

The bonus here is that my toenail polish from Crete, done on June 26th, still looks near on perfect. Even after both feet are broken and I've had an operation on one ankle!

So Nick has just "finished" my wardrobes.

I go to look.

I knew about the missing door, but it transpires that he also has other bits missing still and can't get anywhere near finishing these bloody wardrobes.

I'm seriously sick of this.

And this is all before they have even started on the 2nd bedroom.

I'm so sick of chasing people for a result that I have paid for. It seems all too common these days (I sound like an old person grumbling) that companies don't actually give a monkey's about customer service. It's a massive bug bear of mine too.

I'm going to have to phone the wardrobe company again and I really don't have the energy for it.

Maybe tomorrow.

My wheelchair hasn't arrived yet, not that I was going to use it today. But it would have been a good to have new toy for the day.

Oh, and the really rubbish bit of the day, I fell over.

I tripped over my crutches and twisted my bad leg as I fell onto the poof in the lounge.

The F word came out in front of Iz.

I'm not impressed with myself but I genuinely couldn't help it.

Thankfully she hasn't mentioned it, yet.

My leg is even less impressed than I am. It's killing me. So I've sat with ice packs on it for a few hours to try and reduce any damage.

It seems a bit better after all this but it's definitely stiff and very painful.

I came to bed early as I'm in quite a lot of pain. Iz is snoring like a mini hippo in my bed so I snuggle in next to her - wide awake.

I have to mention this - before I got into bed I told mum about the humungous spider in the bathroom.

The reaction is hysterical….

I've been listening to mum try to get the spider out of the bathroom for ages.

In the end it was hoovered up with the hand held hoover, and the hoover left outside in case the spider crawled out in the house again! (I'll have to get Neil to sort it tomorrow!)

Friday 24th August – wheels and more wheels

No swimming for me today as Mum would rather not take Iz, with me in my state, to a pool that she can't touch the bottom in. I had to tell Iz that my leg hurt too much to swim as she was desperate to go and had really got her hopes up. I hate disappointing her but we'll go next week. She's fine not touching bottom but I totally understand why someone wouldn't want to take her when I'm also on crutches!

It started as a quiet day. I filled my new wardrobes (the bits I could) with clothes – finally!

The temporary rails can go.

The boxes can go.

The bags can go.

And then my wheelchair arrived...woo hoo!

I'm not so sure about it now that it's actually here. I just stare at it for a while.

Also - I'm famous.

Well, my accident and I are. NHS Blood Donation have published my story to raise awareness. I feel really proud of myself as anything I can do to raise awareness for such an amazing cause is worth it. I will share my story with anyone who will listen... hence this book.

NHS Blood Donation   ...
3 hrs

"After 5 transfusions, over 17 broken bones, and multiple internal injuries to my spleen, liver, and carotid artery.... I hear you asking "how are you still here?"

"I ask myself the same question every day. But I also know that our life is about choices, and I chose to breathe on my day. Plus, the help of all the multitude of professionals that piled in on 12th July and the month that followed.

"I had a serious car accident on that morning. Life can change in a split second. I didn't breathe for the time that my car was spinning, and a period after I stopped. But I physically had to tell myself to breathe again. Thank goodness I did.

"But, without those 5 blood transfusions, this would all be worth nothing. I am eternally grateful to all those that have given blood, and those that will in the future. I will do everything in my power to raise awareness, and am writing a book from which the proceeds will go to all the professionals and organisations that helped me.

"The thing that I am most happy for....seeing my 4 year old grow up! She is my world! Here is Iz, to make you all smile 😊."

Back to today:

Physio was great, minus the 28 needles that were nicely placed in my back, knee's, feet, and hands. I'm not so good with needles (I know - wimp), but if it helps my recovery then I'll grin and bear them...and I did today.

Fiona said my foot is good to drive again – yay!

It's kind of a weird feeling being told that you can do something, but feeling completely unready for it physically.

Mentally is a whole different matter. To be honest, I just need to get in a car and drive.

I'll make sure I feel ready physically, and get in as soon as this happens. Otherwise my mental side will stop me doing it if I leave it for too long.

I'm absolutely steaming....I'm in bed at 1830 as I'm so angry.

So, after the great news from Fiona today about driving as soon as I'm ready....

(To put this into context:

It's 7 weeks since my op and accident and I've been told I can drive again by the professionals.

For a normal ankle/leg break etc this is perfectly normal, in fact it's overdue as it's usually 6 weeks)

I've been excelling everyone's expectations and all my bones are healing well. There's no reason at all, once I feel ready, why I can't drive.

You'd be happy for me, right?

Maybe a bit concerned about the impact mentally, but still happy surely?

Wrong.

Neil was delighted and offered me his car for me to drive today. I said no as I don't actually feel ready, but that I hope I do in a week or so when my car arrives.

My mum, however, was not so happy.

In fact, I'd go as far as to say that she was unhappy.

It came out in a conversation where I voiced my concern that some may be concerned about my driving Isabel around in the future. Then my mum decides to say "well you'd be like that if it were the other way around". I know she's right, but I like to think that I wouldn't.

I like to think that I choose who I trust and I stick to it unless it's broken for some reason.

Anyone who looks after Iz is someone that I trust. And I trust their judgement on how to do things. Equally I expect them to trust me and my judgement.

I've even said that I don't feel ready yet for goodness sake!

Sometimes I think that people want me to be a cripple for life (I know they don't really and it's just because they care...but it's how I feel at the moment).

Grrrrrrrrrrrrrrrrrrrrrrr.

* Sorry mum - I love you, I'm just emotional and tired at the time I write this!

Saturday 25th August - all by myself!

So proud of myself – I got in my shower for the first time. And yes, I have had showers since the accident, just not in mine...mine is over the bath and I have to climb in.

But this morning I decided I'd had enough and just climbed in myself.

Now, I make it sound simple .... it did smart ever so slightly.

And it wasn't elegant by any means.

In fact I go as far as to say that it was worthy of a Beadle moment and the £250 prize.

But, I'm clean and my legs are smooth – yes, I shaved them too!

Mum went home for a break after I survived the shower - I've probably sent her grey with stress and worry!

Then I striped my bed on my own, and made it again.

Then I finished putting all my things (more things) away in the new wardrobes.

And then I got a taxi to take me to order my new bathroom and tiles.

Check me! I'm feeling a tad proud of myself - can you tell?!

And now it's time to have my feet done.

I had to let someone near them, although I did warn the lady that I would kick her in the face (in a nice way!!) if she hurt either of them given the number of breaks and the metalwork in there!

Actually she didn't hurt them at all. It was a really nice pedicure. And so it should have been for £50 - ouch. That's more than a luxury spa…and without naming where it was, it certainly wasn't a luxury spa!

On the plus side, I think I might have lost about a stone in dead skin. My feet were disgusting. Now they are significantly better.

I would put a picture in, but you don't really need to see them!

I collapsed when I got home, only moving to get food and wine from the kitchen. Essential items I think you'll find.

Now, it's not as simple as you think to get these items from the kitchen and take them to the lounge when you're on crutches with no hands spare.

So the wheelchair comes into it's own! Wine, glass, and food all on the seat....me and my weight pushing it whilst it holds me upright.

Resourceful right?!

I only managed half my wine (and for those that know me and are reading this - I mean half a glass, not my usual bottle!!) so I've decided - Saturday nights have a new meaning:

Nope, not dancing around crutches....in bed and lights out for 2030....alone!

I actually love it.

I'm beginning to wonder if my accident was life's weird way of telling me that I need to slow down.

Doing nothing is becoming quite appealing, and very unlike me.

I have to say, I'm getting quite concerned. Money is not endless, and my savings are rapidly depleting.

I must think about getting a job! The joke of it is that apparently I shouldn't even consider working until the new year at least. Ha! They must think that money grows on trees!

Now's probably a good time to mention how screwed our benefits system is. So, you get absolutely jack all if you have more than £16k in savings.

So, I earn nothing if I'm sick as I'm self employed and I contract for my work.

And I have to use all my savings to pay my mortgage and living costs.

And when I've done that I may get some benefits as my savings are so depleted, and I will need the system to provide me with housing as I won't be able to afford my mortgage.

Whereas if they helped me with my living costs now and shared some of the load in the first place, then I'd manage to stay in my property and not need them to supply me a house ultimately.

OK, so I should be ok because I will ensure that I have enough money to survive.

But how do other people do it?

What if they're not like me and stubborn as… screwed.

And that's just one part of our system.

Rant over, for now.

I got into bed and for the first time I'm on my own overnight since the accident.

It's been almost 7 weeks…

And just when I thought I was going to sleep, with"All by myself"..Bridget Jones...playing in my head....

Pete messages me to inform me that he'd like Iz on Sunday nights as well on his weekends from September.

Absolutely not!

We had this right at the start of our break up - 20 months ago.

I actually don't have an issue with her spending another night at her daddy's, just not at the moment. We'd have to change the whole schedule to make things work properly for her, and she's been through enough change at the moment! I literally can't put anymore on her. I think she's like me and can take a lot. But she'll get pushed too far at some point.

I had a full on panic attack with my sweats, shakes, nausea, and lack of breath for breathing.

This was not a good combination whilst being on my own for the first time.

At this moment in time I can honestly say that I'm despairing as to what to do. And then I move on to hating myself for letting someone cause me to react like this.

I'm such an arse!

Sleeping pills...all will be better tomorrow.

Sunday 27th August - angels and burden...again!

I woke up feeling much better. Sleep is a medicine in itself for me.

That coupled with my intense stubbornness not to let anything beat me.

Victoria and Sarah came to visit me for the day.

We went for Sunday Roast at the Daffodil in town. It was peeing with rain and we got a taxi in. The taxi driver, unbelievably, sat in the drivers seat and watched as I hobbled out and climbed into the front. I suggested he might like to put my crutches in the boot, and he followed this by watching Victoria take them (in the rain) and put them in.

People are unbelievable.

And in a "service" industry which we pay for.

Wow.

Lunch was lovely, and it was so so good to see the girls. I got a picture too without the crutches!

Love seeing friends as it's so good to laugh. Another natural medicine.

Laughter being a medicine makes me put this in too....

I can't bend down to clear the cat litter at the moment and my mum has been doing it for me. But, given that she was not around, Victoria decided to wheel in and help. I say "wheel in" because she was testing out my wheelchair at the time. So, off she wheeled to the litter tray, and then tried to reach down from the seated position to get the shite, and obviously couldn't reach...you had to be there I guess!

But the point is how much it made us laugh. And I mean belly hurting laughter. That doesn't happen too often and these moments should be cherished.

When we got home after lunch the girls, who I'm now going to call my angels, got into action and we blitzed the house. Sarah washed up whilst Victoria and I sorted upstairs. I cannot explain how much better I feel now that my final box from moving is folded up and in the recycling! My shoes are now safely away in my nice new wardrobe that has shelves for shoes - amazing huh?!

The girls left and I thought Neil was going to be here for tea and Iz's bedtime so I was pretty chilled when she got back from daddy's around 1700.

Ok, so tea was a long shot as he has the boys until 1730...but he'll arrive by 1800, yes?

He's only 8 miles away.

Nope. I got a text from him at 1810 saying he was leaving his in a minute. I told him not to bother as he'll get here at Iz's bedtime, cause mayhem, and be no help at all!

So I did bedtime on my own.

Good thing - I can do it.

Bad thing - absolutely shattered.

My body can't actually cope with this much work in one day yet. And I know it's not much, but I have to acknowledge what my poor body is trying to recover from.

I think I was vile to Neil tonight...in fact, I know I was.

We should all just say what's bugging us when things come up and get it out there. Then we'd talk about it and it would be sorted. Life would be so much easier. And we'd probably have less problems longer term!

Monday 28th August – Time with my baby (not so baby anymore!) girl

Neil and I take Iz out to Eastnor Castle for the day. Oh, and we're taking my wheelchair on it's maiden voyage.

We went to Bathroom Village on the way…it's amazing how much money I can spend when I'm not working – clearly I have too much time on my hands!

And too little money!

I didn't actually spend anything..that comes later. But the principle is there.

On the money note, I've realised that I'm not claiming any spousal maintenance off Pete.

I could be, and probably should be, but it's really not me.

Spousal maintenance is there to help you maintain a house and life for you (and so that you can do this for your child too). I've always maintained that I'm independent and that I will always find a way to pay for myself and my lifestyle. Claiming spousal maintenance just isn't something I want to do.

I actually think I'm a pretty good ex to have…but that's up for debate!

Anyway, back to Eastnor.

Amazing place. Loved it. Absolutely beautiful.

Never have I wanted to go on a bouncy high slide as much as I did today! Probably because there's no way that I can, but it looked so inviting!

Iz didn't want to go on it, even with Neil. They went on the inflatable obstacle course instead.

Iz won – twice!

The wheelchair was ok. It wasn't as adaptable as I thought it would be, but then I didn't spend a fortune on it.

Iz loved riding in it though - both on her own and on my lap!

So - things that I've found out today:

– Eastnor Castle is NOT for wheelchairs! Loads of gravel and hills. I think I did my 10,000 steps on my crutches...let alone if I hadn't been on them!

- Places are generally not geared up for disabled people - steps, everyone using disabled toilets (that was me before), uneven ground, unsuitable entertainment etc

It was truly amazing to go out for the day though.

Neil went and got a curry for mum and I when we got back. Curry, sofa, mum, Neil, and Iz...bliss.

I pushed the boat out and had a chicken korma too...the scales won't be good, but they're not looking brilliant anyway!

16 days until cousin Katy, and Kieran's, wedding... my dress in the wardrobe is looking less and less likely without spanx.

And spanx and crutches are not a good combination I fear....

I have a vision....and let me be clear, it's not a good one!

Tuesday 29th August - work and memories

Woke up feeling a bit down today. Iz is going back to see Daddy for 2 nights and I'm going to miss her terribly. It's nothing unusual in her schedule, but it's the first time I've really felt like this. I think it's his want for more time with her in the future and the uncertainty that comes with it.

So, I spent some time with her before mum took her to pre-school (last week before school starts!) and then waved her on her way.

I made my choice not to let it affect my day though. Again, I could easily feel rubbish but I don't actually want to feel bad. So I am desperately trying not to let my thoughts make me feel like I have to feel that way.

I say it like that as it's not things or people that actually make us feel a certain way, we make ourselves feel like it. It's just easier for us to blame others and circumstances.

The reality is that only we can control the way we think and feel.

It's taken me the last couple of years to really get to grips with this, so I don't for one minute think that it will happen for anyone reading this overnight.

Just think about it though. It's worth it, I promise.

Izzy popped in from Made My Day florists around the corner. She's just driven down the A40 where my accident was and made a good point that I should get some photos of the accident site. I'll go after Sam has been to visit.

Sam and I worked together at Mars for a few years. We're good friends and respect how each other works so it's a good combination. I worked with Sam a few months back in a start up business and we are looking to discuss the same venture again.

We talked generally and it was lovely to catch up.

We also talked 5th Season Fruit and how I could work for them again in the future...fingers crossed, and watch this space.

If I'm involved, you'll all be eating the product before this book comes out!

Neil picked me up at lunchtime so that he could drive me to the A40 and the site where my accident happened. It's only actually 1.5miles from my house. I'd definitely have put it a lot further down the road - at least another few miles. Good job no-one is actually asking me given that I can't remember!

We drove past and then parked up in Capel Lane. We walked over to the site where I now know that I crashed.

There were pieces of my car everywhere.

And pieces of other peoples cars too, that clearly weren't from my accident.

This made me so sad - both from my perspective, but also that it's clearly an accident blackspot that no-one has done anything about to date.

I actually found an earring from my door-well. It was a Christmas one admittedly, but still mine - quite sobering when you see it...

After blubbing on Neil, I thought we should go and see if the site manager or anyone was around on the Dowdeswell Estate.

The site manager was there.

A lovely guy called Rod Jenner. Both him and Chris Gage (Marketing and Comms manager) came over to see us and have a chat.

Rod and a few of his team were first on the scene on the 12th July.

If it wasn't for the fence in place then they would be dead. The wheel that apparently flew off from my car would have wiped about 6 of them out.

It doesn't bear thing about. Thank goodness for the fence.

Neil made a great point that it's an absolute god-send that I was in a 4x4. My car had hit the kerb and grass verges, but it didn't flip over. So thankful.

Rod had 3 first aiders on the scene straight away, and they apparently all headed for the other car after realising that I was kind of talking at that point.

The guy in the other car wasn't in a good way either, and they worked wonders on him whilst waiting for the ambulance.

Oh my god. The poor poor guy. The main impact was apparently on his chest. The main impact on me was all my pelvis.

And this is the benefit of seat-belts. Either your chest or waist/pelvis get the impact of a serious accident - rather than you flying through the windscreen.

Always wear a seatbelt.

I came home and wrote a card to the other driver just to say that I hoped he was managing the pain ok and to say hello.

I still believe that it was a horrible accident which no-one intended to happen, and I hate to think of others being in pain too. I see the pain that just me being involved has caused all of those around me, and thinking of this guy and his family is really distressing.

Tonight sleep is not an option. All I have in my head is how he is and how awful things are for him too.

Note how I'm not thinking of myself at all again. It's like I don't see my injuries at all.

Welcome to my world!

Sleeping pills are definitely not working....

Weds 29th August - shattered

I couldn't move this morning due to no sleep last night.

On the plus side though, I've reduced my medication down by 25% as I've spread them out in the day now – I'm very proud of myself and also remind myself that it's still less than 2 months since the actual accident.

Mum and I had lunch at the Coffee Bean cafe around the corner. Mum met a man called Mark. He's really nice. She was so cool to him. So frustrating as he was clearly interested, even though he apparently has a lady friend...shocking behaviour!

I've spent a couple of hours over at Juliette's this afternoon (over the road). Great to have them all back from their holidays in Germany. Juliette has even baked her hubby a cake to welcome him home from work. I was a terrible wife if this is what I am to compare to!!

When I came home, I got the email from Mum that was her account of the day of my accident - which you will have already read by now.

I cried...a lot.

You probably cried when you read it earlier too - especially if you know my mum and I.

I can't remember many times that my Mum has really told me that she's proud of me.

So when she does, it means a lot to me. And I cry!

Anyway, Neil turned up around 1815ish. He's collected my hair things on the way thank goodness!

It's amazing how much a girl needs her hair products, even with broken bones. I might even make the effort to wash my hair tomorrow before his leaving do from Lloyds, which I've said I will make an appearance at!

So we went to the pub and after we'd had a couple of drinks I brought up the topic of going on holiday as I desperately need some sunshine.

Looks like I've been forgetting conversations.

It's funny because there have been a couple of things recently but I've just ignored them. Now it would appear that they were real things.

Anyway, apparently I've said that I'll pay for a holiday to Thailand for both of us, and for Neil's time off work...classic, considering I'm not earning anything at all and I'm just eating away at my savings, which were supposed to be ring fenced for my house renovation which I'll get on with as soon as I can (both financially and physically).

Hmmm – so 2 weeks in Thailand...£2k, plus 2 weeks off work for Neil £3k...£5k total for Neil alone, highly unlikely!

What am I on??? Aside from codeine and multiple other drugs!!

Obviously this will not be happening. We've compromised and I will pay for us both to go away, but not for the time taken off work.

Thursday 30th August – Sleeping tablets are a crock of ***** - they don't work

I tried them again last night, nothing. No tiredness, no falling asleep, no dreams, nothing....just WIDE awake!

Damn it.

I am so tired! My body is exhausted, and it hurts.

I'll go and see doctor.

My new car arrived today. Wow – it's shiny! Anyone touches it in the driveway and they will have my crutches to contend with!

It's a beautiful black A5 Sportback. No idea when I'll actually drive it, but it's beautiful nonetheless. Loads of toys to play with too....I played for a bit and then went back indoors as mum his due over anytime soon.

Mum and I went together in her car to pick Iz up from her last day at nursery/preschool. I'm actually very sad as it's the end of an era for her, and I to be honest. Iz is not sad at all. She's so excited about starting school in September and all that comes with it that leaving nursery seems a bit of a non-event for her.

I will miss Caroline, Allis, and all the other ladies that work there and have looked after Iz so well over the past year. They have been amazing and really set her up well for school. We'll also miss her friends and their families that we have got to know. But, times change and we all have to move on. There will be new friends and families, and an excellent school to go to!

Friday 31st August - love my cousins!

I've got a new job! I am now the MD for 5th Season Fruit.

Managing Director?!?!

Amazing, and WTF!

I'll have to act like a responsible adult and everything. Hmmm...this could be tricky!

I spoke to my new boss at length and I have until end December to turn things around. Bring it on. I love a challenge.

I'm on it already and I tried to call Sainsbury's - again. I will not give up. The product is amazing and a perfect fit for my favourite supermarket!

I actually really need to get some money in - obviously.

I'm on a mission now.

Charlie, Louisa, and their crew all arrived after lunch - I do love my cousins and it's so nice to see them both and the kids. They are trying to do everything for me and I'm too stubborn to let them.

I haven't seen Louisa since before my accident so it's lovely to catch up properly...and at least she hasn't seen me at my worst - except for the FaceTimes from hospital!

Iz loves having Lily and Maisie to play with, and it makes life so much easier for any parent even at normal times, let alone when I have all these pesky broken bones to contend with!

19.00.

The kids are all in bed asleep.

The wine is on the go.

And chill....

We're all in bed by 2200....

Rock n roll in my life these days! Ah - well, except for Naked Attraction. What is that programme?!

It's near enough porn!! But compulsive viewing! It's hysterical!

Anyway, we're still in bed by 2200 - that's what life has become these days. I need my sleep more than anything, and feel so much better for it.

Bring on the sleep.

Saturday 1ˢᵗ September - Driving!

Loved this morning. The girls (little ones) all played together which was nice, and we took them to the Play Farm in Cheltenham. Great fun. Except for Izzy is going through a phase of not liking noise. I've absolutely no idea where it has come from. She says it doesn't hurt, and that she just doesn't like noise. We'll live with it! I have to say that my tolerance levels are not what they were at the moment...and that wasn't brilliant for parenting a child who is whinging!

We had a pizza at the soft play and then Charlie and Louisa headed off. Next time we see them all will be at Katy and Kieran's wedding in a couple of weeks, with the 3 girls being flower girls...it's so exciting! I can't wait to spin around the dance floor in my chair!!

Neil came over for the afternoon and we chilled with Iz. A bit of a nightmare as Pete couldn't give me a specific time for me to drop Iz at his new place, and Iz really wanted to go there and see her new room, and Daddy of course! It ended up being 1700 in the end, and his whole family were there.

It's the first time since our split that I will have seen everyone.

Oh well, it's right for Iz that we all find a way to see each other and get on.

More importantly though - I drove for the first time since 12th July! I actually got in my car. On my own (my preference). And I drove.

I did drive around Cheltenham first to make sure I was happy with it and that my foot and leg movements were ok and safe. It actually felt good, and the most comfortable I been to be honest. I say that more about physically than mentally. I'm not moving or putting any pressure on my pelvis you see, and the breaks in my feet and leg are healing well so movement is ok.

7 1/2 weeks...not bad, even if I do say so myself!

So "did you actually feel ok mentally?" I hear you all asking...

Yes I did.

Surprisingly.

If I'm really honest, I felt a lot more conscious of what was going on around me, which is actually how we should all act and feel anyway. But if we're honest with ourselves, really honest, we don't.

So, honestly, I've found myself more conscious of both myself and others. But otherwise I'm fine. Thankfully.

Monday 3rd September

I'm staying in bed...sleep is needed more than anything now. I haven't been sleeping as I can't stop thinking about the other driver and whether he is getting better etc. I'm desperate to know how he is, and he's not replied to my card. I do understand this as we are not all the same, but unless he knows something that I don't about what happened, this is a terrible accident that we are both phenomenally lucky to come out of.

On that, I don't see why we can't know how each other is from a legal perspective either. I'm sure there is some GDPR reasoning though!

My sleeping tablets don't work anymore and you've probably gathered that from this book already - except for last night. I think I'm so tired, and I took double dose...whoops. Maybe that's why I still want to sleep at 11am.

Oh, and I can sneeze...you know, properly. Loudly and disturbing for others....woo hoo! Simple things!

Mum is here...she's shattered as usual. Poor mum.

I'm taking Iz with me to Ellen's later so that she can play with Abi and Freya. This will give mum a break too.
I mustn't forget that I have physio tonight..
20.00.....what was I thinking of when I booked this? This is at least pyjama time, if not bed time!! In my new world anyway!

I've got a call with the new business arranged for this Wednesday. My new job is looming...exciting...! The terms are agreed until Christmas. I'm so chuffed as think the business and the product are both amazing.

I will definitely make it work!

And most importantly, it's flexible, so I can make it work around my healing and Iz.

I had some lunch with Iz and then we watched Peter Rabbit in chill time for the zillionth time.

I'm sure I see something new every time I watch it. I still love it though.

And I seriously recommend it if you haven't seen it – adults too!

I took Iz to Sainsbury's with me – she was so proud of mummy walking with the trolley and no crutches in sight! It actually hurts quite a lot, but I'm limited on choices as no-one can push the trolley if I'm on the crutches, with the exception of Iz, and that has limited appeal as I could do with getting home at some point today!!

We only went to the supermarket so as I could collect a parcel of school uniform, but I still came away £65 lighter….online orders only from now on!!

I think my accident has made me more paranoid about the possibility of people hurting themselves….I wouldn't let Iz climb a tree at Ellen's house this afternoon! Even though Abi and Freya were doing it.

Ridiculous.

Steve Magin called me tonight. He was the chief fireman on the day of my accident. It was really good to talk to him. My accident was up there with some pretty tricky ones apparently…I think getting me out proved harder than they wanted!

He is going to come and visit me next week as he lives locally. We are going to see when I can go in and thank everyone. Obviously this will depend on shifts etc, but at least I can drive there now.

On that, I had to ask mum to leave tonight – not as politely as that either…

Unfortunately she admitted that she doesn't trust my judgement when it comes to driving.

I really need support, not people lacking in trust of my decisions and judgement. My consultant and my physiotherapist have both said it's fine so I don't understand why my mum can't be happy for me.

I totally understand her worrying, but she needs to trust me too.

I would never drive if I didn't feel ready. It actually feels like one of the easier things for me to do at the moment, as I've already said!

So, now that Mum has gone home, I'm not sure what on earth I'm going to do re childcare. Tomorrow is going to be challenging. Iz for a full day on my own for the first time since pre 12th July.

Onto Google to figure out what my options are with regards to getting some help.

I meant to say earlier. Someone actually offered to wheel my trolley to the car today...and it was a teenager...my faith is restored!

Mum called.

I didn't speak to her as I think we both need to cool off.

But it's quite simple for me, you have to trust and respect people. If that's not the case, then you can't be together.

Simple.

But life isn't always that simple, is it.!?

Tuesday 4th September - Happy Birthday Geraldine!

Sleep last night was a nightmare...I couldn't get to sleep as my leg was too painful. I actually considered calling an ambulance at one point as I was in so much pain. I'm not sure if it's the lump that has appeared on my right thigh.

The physiotherapist thinks it's a haematoma...not attractive.

Very large, fat like looking lump on my leg. In fact, mum thinks it is fat!

Will see what I can do about it.

Oh, and then I had Iz for the full day.

Really tough.

But I managed...of course!

Sarah came up for a sleepover and put my bins out thankfully. How on earth are you meant to manage when you are incapable of doing certain things like this? I know I haven't researched enough yet, but seriously, there must be more support out there for people? I'm lucky and usually have people around to help me. But there are hundreds of thousands of people on their own, or old, that need support...

Wednesday 5th September - Highs and Lows

Today has been really hard. I could have slept all morning, but realised (with a start) that I had a call with work at 10.00....my new job you see.

I definitely need to get that money coming in.

Sarah was up and we went into Cheltenham so that I could get an outfit that fits for the wedding. I managed to get a dress, hat, and a bag - job done!

Wheelchairs and Sarah - not a good combination... and that's putting it politely! Basically, Sarah nearly killed me - putting it impolitely! Ok, so maybe a slight over-exaggeration...but she nearly tipped me out onto the pavement, and I think my broken bones all went into some kind of seizure!

In Sarah's defence, the pavement was awful, and it was a bumpy bit that we went on. It was actually hysterical...after we'd both recovered from the shock of it!

I'm sure people look at me and think that I shouldn't be in a wheelchair as I can walk a bit and I am generally laughing and looking pretty healthy.

Disabled people must have a nightmare. A whole new world has been opened up to me and I'm fascinated to see how people manage.

I'm actually feeling like a complete burden if I'm honest. I would rather pay someone to come in each day to look after me than someone I love doing it - like my mum, or Neil. I don't want people to help me because they feel they have to or because they feel it's their responsibility to do it. I want them to do it because it's their choice. This is why the having someone who does it for a job is more appealing. At least if I paid someone, they'd more than likely be there out of their own free will rather than thinking of it as a chore.

It's not just my accident that I'm like this with. It's everything. Another example is childcare. I hate being reliant on others, unless I am paying them as it's their choice and job.

So, to make my like easier, and others around me - I'm thinking of buying one of these....what do you think?!

Thursday 6th September - frustration

Today started badly when the wardrobe company failed to turn up, again, to finally finish my wardrobes.

I've lost the plot with them and just want my money back now. I'm going to Trading Standards.

So, based on that start, today was unlikely to go well.

Then I had a bit of a melt down before Neil left.

I blubbed.

Again.

Why is everything so hard? Nothing is straight forward and everything requires a significant effort, even when it should be something simple or something you've paid for.

I'm also still intrigued to know how people on their own manage. Especially if they've got some money in savings.

You get nothing.

NOTHING.

No benefits, no help, nothing.

I know I've said that before, but you can tell that it really really annoys me.

You feel horrendous asking people you know or love.

The only alternative is to pay someone, as above, to be there and help you.

Or you have to find a way to manage.

The worst thing for me is knowing that this is not a short term thing. This is medium term at best. I'm going to be on these god forsaken crutches until the new year probably. And I'm going to suffer for life with pain in cold weather, and probably arthritis in my pelvis when I'm a bit older.

It makes me feel sick to think about it to be honest.

Rant over...back to today.

I looked online and spoke to the CAB about a disabled badge...temporarily. At least until I'm off crutches. I can't even fit my car into a normal car parking space, as I can't open my door wide enough to get in or out...and it's not the size of my arse!

We have a major flaw in our UK system (lots of them!)....so you have an accident and can't walk properly for a prolonged period..but not permanently.

You can't have a disabled badge.

But you can drive.

Where do you park?

Normal spaces....

Aside from the fact that they're tiny, you're also miles away from where you need to be.

Grrrr – this is just one of my bugbears.

Then, this afternoon, thanks to my doctor I'm now back in A&E.

The doctor is really concerned about the lump/ haematoma on my right thigh (attractive I hear you saying). My mum actually genuinely still thinks it's flab as to be honest it does look like this a bit...just in a funny shape and position.

In turn, I've questioned my own judgement about my health because of this!

Nope. It's definitely a lump, and it needs looking at.

So, I'm sat in A&E again.

I'm beginning to know this place really well..and that's not necessarily a good thing.

My doctor specifically requested bed for me as I can't sit still for long periods yet...it's all seats and no beds are available.

I get seen by another doctor pretty quickly. I need an X-ray and an ultrasound. They think it's definitely a haematoma and will leave it alone if so as it's not causing me too many issues at the moment.

Great - I look like a freak with a lump on the side of my leg. And I'm actually no further forward than I was this morning at home. I've just wasted an afternoon.

If it stays as it is I'll never be able to wear leggings again...at least Iz will be pleased as she hates me in leggings!

Ok, so I'm finally home at 1900 and someone really lovely has left me a gorgeous bunch of flowers on my doorstep. It's not Neil, so I'm trying to figure out who the lovely person is.

They've brightened my day up so I'm very grateful.

Pete dropped Iz back and she is snuggled in my bed as I type. She's waiting for mummy to snuggle in with her. It won't be long tonight. I'm shattered after being on my feet for most of today.

Mum is coming over tomorrow. It's the first time since our "run in" earlier in the week. I'm still not sure how I feel about it all, but Iz can't wait to see Grandma so that's good.

I also can't believe that Iz's new teacher is coming over tomorrow, and Iz starts proper grown up school next week. My little baby is starting school.

Enough said!

Ooooh – get to climb into bed at 2130. Bliss....

There's a bit of a problem though....

Friday 7th September

Hurrah – Iz slept until 0715!

Mum arrived with us just after 0900...neither of us mentioned anything about earlier in the week so we just got on with it. I suspect it will remain that way.

Pete arrived at 1020 as we have Iz's new teacher coming over today – it's the right thing for us to be a family unit for this.

But it's hard.

I'm sure Pete feels the same!

The teacher meeting was good, and you could be forgiven for thinking we were just a normal 2:4 children family. We behaved very well.

I then received a text later in the day asking for my solicitor details so that he can progress the action for changing the night routine with Isabel. ....I can't believe that he is doing this. And now of all times. I'm literally at a loss as to what to do as I have no energy to fight it all.

All of my energy is going into fixing myself for my little girl.

It did make me worry about the future though. I have no absolutely no idea what the future holds - financially, physically, or mentally.

Not a great place for me to be in.

And then....

Oh my goodness! I'm famous! I'm in the Mail Online!!

I actually don't like the paper at all, but the readership is huge so it's the best one to be in for impact and raising awareness of NHS Blood Donation and GWAAC (Great Western Air Ambulance Charity).

My article has been shared nearly 200 times by the end of the day.

Amazing to think how many people this has reached, and all from little ol' me.

So far, we have NHS Blood Donation and The Daily Mail :)

My work here is ongoing. If I'm going to do anything, I'm going to deliver something good from something so horrific.

Mother, 42, who survived a horror car crash recalls her near-death experience - and how she saw herself 'running free through fields' as she was cut from the wreckage

By Unity Blott For Mailonline
Updated at 09:09 on 7 September 2018

49 shares   1 comment

- Mother-of-one Emily Pringle suffered a horrific crash in Cheltenham on July 12

Saturday 8th September - Judging people by own standards....

Don't do it!! Just because you may do or say something, doesn't mean that others will too.

The reason I say this....I sent my article from yesterday's Daily Mail to 67 people on email last night.

67.

I got 10 replies in total (retrospectively updated).

Wow. I am constantly truly baffled as to how people handle things.

I'm trying to raise awareness and money, and bring something good out of a really horrific situation. And to help others in the process.

And people don't react.

All I have to assume is that they have different ways of dealing with things.

I can't influence how anyone else thinks or feels....only myself. I have to keep telling myself this.

Anyway, I'm literally speechless (for a while!).

Back to today.

The plan was to have a little bit of a lie in, especially given that mum is here.....

Iz decides to wake up at 0600....joy! She then proceeded to talk to me at great length in between Horrid Henry and Elena of Avalor until 0715 when I told her to go and wake Grandma up!!

I thought I might get left in peace then...but no!

So I got up and packed stuff for our weekend away at Auntie Sarah's. Iz is super excited to see Grace and Eva later today (Sarah's nieces). And we've just found out that it's Daisy's birthday and we're seeing her tomorrow. Now she's really excited!

We met Daisy and her family on our holiday in Crete. They are from Maidenhead, where we used to live. I can't believe our paths haven't crossed at all in 40 years! Our holiday was made by meeting these guys and we had a really good time. Not to mention the fact that Iz and Daisy were like 2 peas in a pod.

We promised we'd catch up when we got back, and we're doing it. Accident in the way, no way!

I drove us down to Sarah's in the afternoon - it's the furthest I've driven so far - and spent some time with the girls before Iz went to bed. Then we just chilled. Boy did I need it after the drive.

It's actually also the first time I've stayed away from home too since I got back after my accident early August.

I'd be lying if I said I wasn't concerned about not being in my own bed, but there's no better place than Sarah's to start. And it was very comfortable.

Sunday 9th September - Friends

Today was special. Special because it was chilled. Special because we were in our hometown. Special because we popped in to see my Aunt & Uncle, and got them plus 2 of my cousins with Lily & Henry too (Iz's cousins). And special because Iz and I met up with the great friends that we made whilst in Crete, pre all the rubbish that has happened.

It was amazing to see Emma, Jon, Daisy and Charlie. We chilled at theirs whilst the kids played together. It brought it all back explaining to them what had happened. And it was really weird given that the last time I saw them we were prancing around in a swimming pool with not a care in the world. We will definitely all stay in touch, and hopefully next time I'll be a bit more mobile!

Monday 10th September – nada!

Literally nada.

Nothing to report.

Drugs, food, sleep, drugs, food, sleep.

Tuesday 11th September – trust

Or lack of....

So apparently I'm the talk of the village....

It's amazing what people choose to gossip about, and they always want to believe the worst possible scenarios.

I was mortally offended when I found out that I was the topic of conversation in numerous places. Lots of people discussing the accident and the why's and wherefores.

As if they were all there.

And they are the pro's.

I've put a post on FB and LinkedIn to try and rectify as much as I can.

On another note, the press is going a bit mad...

So I had Femail on Friday.

Gloucestershire Live today.

AND ITV West Country want to do a face to face! Eeek....I'd best make myself look a little more respectable and get dressed when they come over.

I literally can't believe how much awareness I can raise through these channels. I just want to help those that saved me.

I want to donate blood, but I can't due to the 5 transfusions. I want to give money to the GWAAC, but I can't always afford to.

So I'll have to support them in another way, and that's exactly what I'm doing.

Back to today....

I've realised that lying on my right side (injured side) has become a bit of a thing that I do now....I actually don't really notice myself moving into that position anymore, and I can get back again without some kind of hoist or other contraption!! I have to point out that I only manage it for about 5 minutes at a time! But it's progress.

On a not so good note, the pain in my left leg has ramped up to another level now. It seems to have shifted down a few centimetres and I've had it at least 10 times in last 24hours...

I probably had it 10 times in last month previously. I have spoken to the doctors and they have increased my dose of Gabapentin...I'm not sure it will help though. They said not to worry as I'm seeing the neurologist next week anyway. I didn't like to say that I'll be in A&E before that happens if the pain continues like this!!

Drug count - up again! Damn it!

Wednesday 12th September - no tears!

Isabel's first day at school.

Emotional, but no tears from either of us and great to see them all off on their first day of their new adventure. She was so brave!

There's only 6 of them starting today.

Classroom set up ready. Loads of games.

It reminded me of being back in school. Amazing.

Pete was there too as it's definitely right for Iz to have both of us with her for this day. I cooked lunch for them both - Lasagne. It's apparently Iz's favourite. She has a new favourite every time she has a meal. Kids!

After school ITV came to interview me - yes, interview me - get me! I'm going to be famous! Ha! Film crew and everything.

Oh god, thank goodness they gave me 5 mins to find my makeup. I looked rough as. And it absolutely IS true that a camera adds the pounds!! Definitely!

But we did it, and Ken will call me tomorrow to let me know how it all looks.

More publicity for the amazing teams that saved myself and the other guy.

Neil and I are off to see the Full Monty tonight at the Everyman Theatre in town. I can't wait. I'm not sure whether Neil is as excited as me! Probably not given that the men will be getting their kit off on the stage.

Hmmm....he can get ice cream at this point!

And they did get their kit off ladies!!

And I got to meet them all afterwards...amazing!

The guys all donated money for the Air Ambulance, and we got to go for drinks with them. It really doesn't get much better than this! (I'm thinking back to my Hollyoaks watching days as I type this...and I know some of my friends will be shouting that I still watch it...ok, so maybe I do, occasionally!)

Gary Lucy doing a dab, with a crutch!! Very cool (to all the kids out there!).

Thursday 13th September - NEVER forget drugs again

Ok, so I had too much to drink last night...but it was exceptional circumstances.

But, I forgot my tablets when I went to bed and I couldn't move for the first 3 hours this morning.

I have never felt pain like it.

I literally couldn't move at all.

So, not a good day – which is obvious from the above I know, but actually not good generally.

I felt really down about things overall. Crutches, tablets, pain, metalwork....everything.

To be honest, I think I've done pretty well so far. The only "down" day I've actually had was the day the police came around...earlier in this book.

2 days out of 63 isn't a bad stat considering what my poor body has been through.

Anyway, that's how today started.

Then I got the call to listen through my ITV News article....tear jerking.

Seriously tear jerking.

Bless Ken Goodwin though - he actually wanted to check with me that I was ok with everything before sending it off as he knew how traumatic it had all been.

Then I missed my first team call as the MD of 5th Season Fruit. Not a good start!

And then, on top of what was shaping up to be a pretty crappy morning, my ex mum in law called me.

Marvellous.

I was actually thinking "it doesn't really get much better than this" at this point.

But, it was really nice to talk to her as it's been ages. And I love her to bits. I do miss her lots. I just couldn't deal with speaking to her on the day that I'm feeling a bit rubbish...more tears. She must think I'm a total weirdo.

Lunchtime – it's my new start to the day!

And it needs to be as I need to get some work done!

You'll be pleased to know that my afternoon was really productive, after my slow start.

Another thing I need to mention....

Paperwork. Mountains of it.

Does everyone suffer like this or just me?

I'm talking bills, letters, school stuff etc ....

And that's before I even start on any work!

Friday 14th September - Happy times

Wedding day for my middle cousin - Katy, and her fiancé Kieran.

A truly amazing day, and Iz was a flower girl. I'm so proud of all the kids involved as they were superstars for the day, and they all kept going until well after 2100. There were no meltdowns. No tantrums. I know, I know - "exactly as kids should be" I hear you say, but the reality is that they are generally not like this! So it was a pleasant surprise.

Iz disappeared with her cousin Lily, and Joshua, who is a friend that she has taken a particular shine to...in addition to Lewis from Crete :) They were gone for most of the day...entertaining each other.

Me however, I was in the wheelchair by 1600. My heels did me proud though and I made it until then on them!

It's amazing how much champers you can drink once in a wheelchair!

Such a lovely wedding. Katy, and Kieran so happy and in love.

A beautiful day.

Iz headed off to bed with Grandma at about 2130 and we thought we'd get the party started.

By 2230 though I had had it. I hated the fact that I had to ask Neil to take me to bed...not in the nice way, but because I couldn't walk there myself. Our room was miles away, but to be honest it could have been much nearer and I'd still have needed the chair.

He wheeled me back and made sure that I got into bed ok. I wondered why he wasn't making any attempt to get ready for bed himself...and then all became apparent when he went back out to the wedding and the bar again!

So, I lay in bed like a true cripple. Sorry for the use of the word, but that's what I felt like.

I couldn't move and I couldn't do anything about it. I was totally reliant on others.

For some reason I felt claustrophobic.

Stupid as that sounds as the bed was the biggest bed I've ever slept in.

But because the pain in my "good" leg is back, I definitely can't lie on my side. So I'm stuck on my back with limited movement.

You can see why the claustrophobia is kicking in.

Saturday 15th September - Pain and rough

Enough said.

I think I've been doing too much. And I know everyone will be screaming at this book that "of course I have".

I'm so stubborn though, and I keep going. I've never been in this position before.

I rarely even get a cold so I can't compare it to anything in my life.

But my body is definitely telling me to stop. And to stop now.

We all had breakfast with the wedding party, and after the kids had played for a while, I waved Iz off for the rest of the weekend with Daddy. Daddy came to collect her so it was nice for him to see everyone too...they were his family too for years.

Neil and I headed back to Cheltenham for a chilled afternoon - well, as chilled as clearing the conservatory is. (And I know I'm meant to be doing nothing!)

Sunday 16th September - Relapse

Or that's how it felt.

I couldn't really move.

Enough said.

Monday 17th September - Physio pain

Acupuncture....needles everywhere!

The nerve pain in my leg is apparently coming from my back. Fiona thinks it may be where one of my vertebrae is healing and rubbing against the nerve. I just need to get the pain under control. It's literally every time I move.

It happens when I'm standing up. And when I touch it. Neither of which were happening when I first got it. That was just when I sat in a certain position.

I'm seeing the neurologist tomorrow so I'm going to talk to him about this too. The actual reason I'm going to see the neurologist is for a pain in the side of my head that I've had since the accident, which I thought it was a bruise when I felt it in the hospital when I was being treated.

But it's not gone, so unlikely to be that.

Now I have 2 things to talk to him about.

Oooh – on another note. I'm on television tonight. ITV News for West Country at 1800. 3.5minutes too...much longer than most articles, they apparently only last for 2.5minutes.

I came across ok I think. And I didn't look too horrific - the make up definitely helped.

As I said earlier, the camera most definitely adds the pounds - I looked like Jaba!

Now...where are those custard creams?

Ah – I finished them earlier!

There's a reason that I'll never be skinny, and I'm glad because it actually works for me.

I could just do with losing a few pounds though....like 28 of them!!

Tuesday 18th September – Neurology

The pain has been incredible all day. As Mr Silva said to me tonight – unless someone has suffered from neuro pain then they won't know what it feels like. It's truly horrific. I have cried at least 4 times today because I've either been stuck in bed, on the sofa, or on the toilet...not the most glam.

My last instance was on the toilet downstairs at home, just after the builders doing my upstairs bathroom had left for the day.

I literally couldn't move once I was on the toilet. I couldn't move my legs, my arms, my hands.

Nothing.

And I couldn't wipe my bottom (not nice) - thankfully it was only wee, and not poo!

I couldn't lift either leg, and I couldn't move my feet.

Seriously nothing.

I certainly couldn't get up. I was screaming in pain. And I mean screaming. We're not talking a little yelp. We're talking full on out loud.

I'm sure the neighbour heard me - and she's in her 80's.

I must have had the searing burn pain at least 8 times in this instance. I was nearly sick it was so horrific.

I thought I was going to have to stay there until the morning when Matt and Rob turn up just before 08.30 to continue doing the bathroom. They'd have to kick the front door down and find me with my knickers around my ankles. Nice.

Things weren't looking good, and my appointment at the hospital was looming in the evening.

So I had to man up and stand through the pain. And boy was there pain.

But I did it.

And I blubbed.

A lot.

It was actually only 1715 when I looked and I didn't need to be at my appointment with the neurologist until 1840 (20 mins away), but I just needed to get there now. The pain was actually scaring me in a way. And this has now completely taken over my need to get my head sorted.

I felt that if I was in the hospital and it happened again, at least they would know what to do!

I got there and waited. The burning was there but it wasn't shooting up my leg like earlier so I could cope.

Mr Silva was amazing.

The pain is my lateral femoral cutaneous nerve.

Check me! I actually looked it up as I had forgotten the name!

For those that can't be bothered to look it up, it's the nerve that passes through your groin and down the outside of your left leg.

Pain here can be caused by trauma, tight clothes, or obesity. But a change in something. There has been no change since my accident that I'm aware of.

I balled on Mr Silva when he said he couldn't solve it tonight.

I'm needed back tomorrow though to see the pain specialist. Mr Silva called him as I left and asked him to fit me in to his clinic no matter what.

They wanted to admit me for the night, but actually they can't give me any different drugs to those that I'm taking anyway, so there's no point.

And I've got no-one at home to look after Jess the cat.

Home it is.

Re the head issue that I actually booked the appointment for in the first place...I need an MRI of the brain.

So, back for more scans, MRI's, X-Rays, and drugs.....definitely drugs.

I'm going to bed now...2118.

More drugs, and sleep.

The bathroom guys are coming at 0830!

Wednesday 19th September - pre-op, or not

What I forgot to say yesterday, was that I'm famous! A random man came up to me outside the café in Charlton Kings yesterday to ask if I was the girl on the TV the previous night!! He he!!

After my brush with fame at lunchtime today, I went to see an amazing consultant called Paddy Clarke in the afternoon...not quite my namesake, but close enough. He is a pain specialist. This was prioritised over my pre-op appointment as I can barely move!

Neil came with me and I couldn't even get out of the car without an "episode".

Nightmare.

Anyway, Paddy had a look – I've no pride left AT ALL since my stint in hospital so I was more than happy to take my kit off for him!

He agreed with Mr Silva about where the pain is coming from and said that there was no point in doing the injection as he needs to find the cause of the pain first, and also the injection only actually lasts 24hours.

I totally understand, in my rational mind. But this is my irrational mind at the moment...

Oh my goodness – I seriously can't cope much more. Out come the tears again.

He sent me for an x-ray as wants to look at the metalwork in my pelvis - specifically the scaffolding that's due out on the 9th October....ah ha...it's moved.

Admittedly only a couple of millimetres, but that is enough apparently.

So that's what causing the pain. He is 99.8% certain. That's good enough for me!

He has taken me straight off the codeine that I've been on since July – which apparently doesn't work after 8 weeks anyway – no bugger told me that!

So I've been taking a drug that people get addicted to, for no reason...marvellous. I love the fact that my doctors just keep putting it on repeat prescription and not questioning it at all!

I've been switched onto Tramadol which is apparently very good for nerves. Paddy trebled my dose of Gabapentin. Hmmm – I haven't worked it out but I think my total tablets in a day has now gone up again!

My only knowledge of Tramadol is not good knowledge – sickness and addiction. And Paddy told me that it can interfere with other medication that I'm on to cause edginess and sweating – attractive traits! Can't wait for those then!

Anyway, off home with a new set of instructions and left Paddy Clarke phoning Mr Achyara to see if he can bring my operation forward at all.

I don't think that's going to happen as I'm sure he's not available the week before but we'll see.

Neil and I went out as I thought it may be my last opportunity for a couple of glasses of vino for a few weeks. Alcohol and Tramadol are not brilliant together...it intensifies the side effects of Tramadol...this could be messy!

Unfortunately Neil and I didn't have the best evening. We got onto money and kids...neither of which we are aligned on. He doesn't have the spare cash that I spend (out of my savings), and his kids are influenced by his ex...and we think they are told to ignore my daughter. I can't expose her to this. So him and I need some conversations on our future.

It's not for tonight, I definitely do not have the capacity at the moment.

Thursday 20th September - drugs drugs drugs

The pain is still there but nowhere near as bad. It's still stabbing, but then goes off after a few seconds, so the drugs are definitely working.

I'm concentrating on my new drug regime today, so I'm not writing any more.

Friday 21st September - Wardrobe shelves but no door!

And you thought that was all done!!

Anyway, Iz was dropped at school, and the wardrobes in my room had their 4th visit - and they're still not finished! Poor Nick who is fitting them. Even he is embarrassed by the lack of Customer Service that I have received.

On the plus side, I got my deposit back today from my old house. It's been in a dispute with the DPS and I stood to lose £2,000. But I got the whole lot back as they ruled in my favour.

Amazing. Things do go my way!!

Iz had a playdate at her friends house after school. it was lovely and killed several hours.

After we got home, Iz and mum left to go to Grandma's for a sleepover so that I could have a bit of a break.

Peace at last!

House to myself.

Glass of red.

Bliss.

I've doubled my dose of Tramadol as the pain is slightly worse today and I'm only taking half the maximum dose. Hopefully this will stop the pain altogether.

I popped over to Ellen and Jason's and had a takeaway with them, with more wine.

No adverse effects thank goodness.....until the night-time in bed....sweating!

Sheets drenched!

Eeewww!

I'm so glad I had the bed to myself!

Oh - just as a note. Whilst all this is going on with the pain, MRI's, X-rays, ultrasounds etc... I now have to look at mediation for this extra night business for Isabel with Pete.

I could do without this.

She is the most important thing to me on the planet, but it can wait surely?!

Saturday 22nd September - Tweedy the Clown

Bloody pain is still there.

It's even bad when I'm lying in bed early in the morning. My left leg just gets the stabbing pain whenever I move.

I've never had it when lying down so this is a new thing in the last few days.

It was really bad when I got up today too. When I stood up out of bed, it was agony.

I'm going to see what it's like tomorrow, and then it might be back to Paddy Clarke on Monday if it's still bad. Not that I think they can do anything. I think I'm maxed out on medication and I just have to wait for my operation in 2.5 weeks.

Anyway, better than talking about pain – we went to the circus today.

Gifford's Circus in Cirencester.

It was fabulous!

We went last year so we knew what to expect. But the crutches also help you to get on the front row – brilliant!

It pee-ed with rain again (did this last year too).

Got drenched!

Iz loved the circus and Tweedy the Clown in particular. I think she's high on sweets too... parenting at it's best...again!

As a result, Izzy was a nightmare tonight.

She was dog tired.

She's got a cold.

And she was late to bed.

Great combo!

I've sent mum up there to sort her now as I can't do anymore today!

I'm on the red again. I'm not an alcoholic...I promise!

Sunday 23rd September - Me and Iz

I've had such a nice day. And I've spent most of it with Iz. Just her and I for the first time in ages. OK, so I can't do all that I used to do, but we can still do some things.

We went swimming this morning. Iz swam a whole length of the pool...and beat me! Suffice to say that I can't swim properly as yet! I carried her down the length of the pool on my back at one point. I probably shouldn't have done this as, although it didn't feel like anything in the pool, it did afterwards!

More drugs needed!

When we got home we got to make crumble and cakes...Iz loved it!

The final episode of The Bodyguard tonight....

Personally I thought it was a bit of a naff last episode and I was a little disappointed after sitting on the edge of my seat (as much as possible) for the last few weeks!

I went to bed disappointed.

Monday 24th September – I'm a Managing Director

And this is our business (not mine and Sarah's - that's the other one!). I genuinely love it. I give the products to Iz and anyone that comes over to our house. They are great for kids and for adults.

Tuesday 25th September - 2 weeks to go!

So, 2 weeks and then some of this metalwork comes out!

Hurrah!

I get to go down to 1 crutch and learn to walk again...this could be interesting!

Not that I'm counting...much.

I had a big meeting in London today to meet some of the Convenience guys that we want to work with on 5th Season Fruit. We're taking them out for lunch to wine and dine them and glean lots of feedback from them on our products.

120miles...7hours.

I left home at 0745. Got to Oxford at 0915. And then to the outskirts of London around 1000.

And then The Folly restaurant at 1230.

WTF ?!? Ok, so I had to park too...but seriously?!

It goes down as one of my best days...for enjoying my own company! At least I have a nice new car!

Gill cooked me a lovely dinner this evening and I had 2 glasses of wine.

I'm shattered now.

My accident has brought Gill and I closer, but we still need to spend time together to get back to where we were previously.

Wednesday 26th September - treats!

A new MacBook - all for me! I'd better figure out how to use the flippin' thing!

Mostly on my Divorce business today.

It's quite therapeutic and also my accident has taught me to view things a bit differently. Life is too short to spend time on things that aren't all that important to us.

I prioritise a lot more now, and I back down on the things that take a huge amount of energy but aren't necessarily worth it in the grand scheme of things.

It's worth thinking about...

To help….draw the following and put all of your to do list in the boxes. Then challenge yourself to scrap (either temporarily or permanently) things in the not urgent or not important boxes …. it's enlightening I promise.

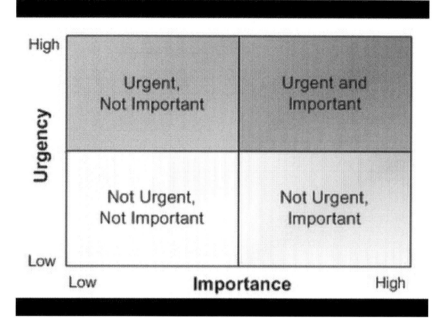

Thursday 27th September - All by myself

So, last night Neil and I kind of broke up.

Why? I hear you say. Perfect couple, recovering from operation etc..

We'll have to see what happens.

Unfortunately timing is not on our side, and drunken conversations led us to this conclusion.

Both of us want to live as one happy family, but neither of us can see it with our families put together as it stands. Our kids don't get on and we have his ex's influence to deal with.

That's life .

So I now feel like Bridget Jones – All by myself!

Anyway..onwards and upwards.

I've done it before and I'll do it again. Admittedly I wasn't 11 weeks post almost dying, with a 4 year old in tow. But I'll be fine.

Choices again!

So – what shall I do with my first single day in 10 years?

Work!!

Oh, and my rescheduled pre-op is later.

It feels weird going to Southmead Hospital again. It feels a bit like home.

I say that in the sense that it feels safe. I feel safe there. It's like I feel at the Winfield when I go there for appointments. There's a safety feeling and I can only assume it's because they looked after me at my worst time in these places.

There's no other reason that I can come up with.

I did have a minor panic attack when I was leaving Southmead.

I've no idea why.

Life goes on in other places but I didn't want to leave.

I feel exceptionally lonely at the moment, and it's not just my newly founded single life.

Iz is at daddy's this weekend. Mum is going home, and I don't talk to her about "stuff" at all. And Neil and I have split up.

I feel very odd.

On the plus side...I can feel my right leg again!

This is MAJOR!

I never thought this would happen, but 11 weeks on and I can feel my right thigh again.
I actually think the left one may be coming back too.
I had forgotten what it felt like to have feeling in my thighs!

Friday 28th September – All by myself

Actually the case, for the first time in an AGE...10 years to be precise.

I'm not sure that it actually feels good. Neil has been my rock through the accident, and before it to be honest.

My bathroom fitters have also gone now. And the skip is gone!

I'm now worrying about money. My savings are dangerously low and I earn no money. And I have no other income. I can't get any benefits as I have some savings, even though they are low.

But seriously, I don't actually know what I'm going to do. I am working, but no pay until December as that's what we've agreed on. And it's actually longer term that I'm thinking of.

My lifestyle is going to have to change somewhat.

I know I've booked a holiday etc (might have forgotten to mention that - Dubai mid Oct!), but things are going to have to get very tight around here. No more treats for a while.

I'd better turn 5th Season Fruit into a massive success and get some money from it!

It must be a good time to plug the business again - check it out!

Saturday 29th September - Decisions

Now vs 10 years ago - almost to the day:

Then....no broken bones....no operation on the horizon.
Able to walk, run, cycle...anything.
I lived in stable area with friends on tap.
Family on tap.
Work on tap.
Rented a house in Marlow...young free and single!

Now...none of the above admittedly, and still a lot of broken bits to contend with, but...
A daughter with me half the time.
A house of my own.
A pussycat to look after.
Living in Cheltenham.
A brand new swanky bathroom in my house.
Friends close by.

Life is not that bad :-)

So I have a choice, again...

I can lie here feeling sorry for myself and crying...

OR

I can get my sorry backside out of bed (still like Bambi I'm afraid) and get on with sorting my amazing new bathroom, and wardrobes etc. Maybe I'll pop into town and see what's going on there over a coffee. And maybe I'll pop over to Ellen's as I know she has a houseful for Freya's bday.

Now that I've had my few hours of pity for myself... I'm going for the 2nd option!

Drugs update - I'm still on them!
But, only 24 tablets per day, which is significantly less than a few weeks ago.

It's still 24 more than I want though!

I actually felt good when I finally got out of bed.

I text Neil and asked him if we could talk. Surely we've given up too easily. As he said, we're trying to predict the future. We're the first ones that should know that you can't do that! My accident should tell anyone that. Things can change in an instant.

So we've decided to try again. But we're doing things differently. We're doing things together, with the kids, and with our families.

After this was sorted I actually went into Cheltenham for the first time properly and had a wander around. Well - a wander as much as you can wander on crutches. What this actually consisted of was visiting 2 stores and then sitting in a bar having a glass of vino whilst waiting for Neil to come and pick me up!

Then we just went to the local for a few drinks and a bite to eat.

2 women on the next table were talking about 1 of them leaving her husband..I obviously gave my business details to her (not the fruit business, the other one!)

I might as well plug that one here too!! It's a business designed to help individuals through their separation or divorce. We help with emotional and practical support throughout the process. I help clients gain clarity on what they want, and what position they are likely to be in coming out of the other side. I am ultimately a coaching business, but with significant experience in the legal process and the emotion that comes with losing someone.

The Divorce Partner - new business taking over from Absolute Clarity, but in purely my name.

Sunday 30th September - sleep zzzzz

Literally....zzzzzzz.....

Monday 1st October - It's October!!

I can't actually believe it's October already.

Anyway...as I lie in my bed cuddling Iz whilst lying on my side for a period of time, for the first time since my accident, I remember that it wasn't so long ago that 4 nurses had to put me on my side every 4 hours to make sure I didn't get bed sores and to make sure my wounds were ok.

Wow.
How things change so quickly.

So, as I come up to my 12 week anniversary, and the removal of my pelvic scaffolding...these are some of the things that I used to take for granted, that I now feel eternally thankful for:

Walking (albeit on crutches still!).
Carrying things (um, sort of whilst trying to balance on said crutches!).
Going to the toilet - yep, without a catheter and without a mountain toilet seat!

Cooking a meal - I actually cooked for the first time yesterday.
Putting make up on - admittedly I don't do as often anymore.
Showering - thankfully a regular occurrence now.

And the main one....
Cuddling!
My little girl, my partner, my family and friends. Everyone!

So, I still can't bounce out of bed, walk without crutches, lie on my front, sleep on my side, get up without feeling and looking like a 90 year old, or go out dancing after a few vino's ...but give me time!

And I'll still never run a marathon...but that was never going to happen anyway so all is good in the world.

We should never take for granted the fact that we are here, or what we can do.
Things can change in an instant. We are exceptionally lucky. And I certainly feel it x

I had both physiotherapy and hydrotherapy today...

I think the hydrotherapy is helping massively because last week I definitely noticed a difference in how my muscles and bones felt for several days after doing it.

I've actually been walking without my crutches... but I'm not meant to.

Can you imagine how frustrating it is...being able to do something but not being allowed to? And I don't mean like it was when we were kids...this is something now that has serious repercussions if I do it, it will impact my future.

It's a nightmare.

I do understand. I'm not meant to weight bear on my pelvis until 12 weeks post my initial operation, so it will be worth it.

I'm trying really hard to make sure that I'm using them all the time, but sometimes I forget. Don't get me wrong...it's not easy to walk without them, and every bone and muscle screams at me when I do so. It's just sometimes I forget that I can't walk...if that makes any sense!

Getting out of bed is getting easier too. I'm still like bambi, but I can get my legs out the side without too much trauma now.

Tuesday 2nd October

Manic - as usual!

After dropping Iz at school, I raced over to Gloucester for a client meeting, before heading for an MRI of my head and back.

This is for the "bruising" that I can feel on the side of my head since the accident. It hasn't faded with time and I need to get it checked as it's worrying me. I'm also not convinced that there was a complete scan of my head done at the time of my accident.

The MRI tunnel.....really looking forward to it....not!

I sat in the waiting room at The Winfield.....and then it was cancelled! Just as I had got there and sat down to relax. Slightly annoying, especially given that I had drugged up for the claustrophobia feeling and I now had to sit in reception for a couple of hours to let the weird feelings pass.

Hey ho, more time to head down to Windsor to meet some of my old team for dinner and drinkies. It was so good to see them all.

Obviously I got absolutely trashed and can't remember getting to bed....standard....except for the fact that I probably had half the alcohol that I

would have had on previous nights out with them.
...I'm just taking meds that make up for it now.

Wednesday 3rd October

On the eve of the 12 week anniversary for my accident...I found myself sat in the school hall this evening and realised that the last time I was sat there was exactly 12 weeks ago...on the eve of my accident.

Who'd have known what was going to happen 14 hours later....
And I have to say it was the most strange feeling, but I held it together....just...

Today has been a strange day anyway.

We had a great team meeting with the amazing 5th Season team, but I'm feeling really low for only the 3rd time since my accident. I know it's only the 3rd time as I know exactly when the other 2 times have been...earlier in here!

I'm exceptionally lucky as somehow I've managed to look on the positive side throughout my recovery to date.
However, I felt the need to highlight a message that I learnt when I suffered with post natal depression:

"It's ok not to be ok"

But, for me, it's really important to bring myself back to feeling ok again. Otherwise I will get into a spiral.
And I do understand how easy it would be to get into that spiral, and I understand how this can happen to people.

But for now, and for me, it's back to ok...after some sleep!!

Thursday 5th October - Epic fail

I thought I'd be smart and reduce my drugs. So, I went from 24 per day down to 16, in one go. I still take them 3 times per day, but 1 less of each tablet...

Hmmm...I'm hurting by lunchtime. But it could be anything, right?!

I'll persevere....

I'm in agony by the evening.

So it's back to the full dosage for now.

I'm not going to write about it being the 12 week anniversary as I said enough yesterday, except for the reason for the importance of 12 weeks....it's when I can start putting my full weight on my pelvis again...

i.e Walking with no crutches, and not harming myself!

So in my eyes it's when I can start to get my body back to normal - whatever normal might be for me now!

Friday 6th October - Reality hits

Today started off really well.

I had some brekkie with Iz and then did the school run.

Had a gossip with Jo at the school gates - not about me for a change - and headed home for a cuppa.

I had a lovely clean house (thanks Sam!).

My washing was done.

And I did some work.

Then I got to see John, my first boss in the world of FMCG. And, more importantly, my first boss in the world of chocolate!

It was great to see him. And it was still the same as ever! AND he bought me chocolate - love him to bits!

I will not love him when I put my bikini on in a few weeks for Dubai!!

The reason I say reality hits as my title for today, is that John commented on all I'm doing at the moment....

Absolute Clarity

5th Season Fruit

Mummy to a 4 year old

Girlfriend

New home owner

and most importantly, recovering from a very serious car accident in which I nearly died.

Sobering huh?!

I actually already knew all of this, and had kind of been thinking about it for a few days. I just chose not to do anything about it.

Anyway, as I type this, my mum has gone to get Iz from school to try and help me.

She will have Iz for me this afternoon but, to be honest, if they're in the house it's not really a break. Iz just wants to be with her mummy at the moment - understandably. And it's my weekend with her too.

Thank goodness Pete and I have swapped our Sundays for this week. I get a day to myself then - phew!

I have to say though, being a single parent, I feel that I need to spend all the time I have Iz with me, with her...if that makes sense? I know that you'll tell me this is ridiculous and not possible, but it's the way that I feel.

GUILT.

And kids love to make us feel bad don't they?! Iz can be very good at this!

So I did spend time with her this afternoon after school, and it was lovely.

But then nightmare child appeared out of nowhere....it was the WORST bedtime ever.

And then I went to bed at 2100 after Izzy woke up coughing and in tears. She wanted to come into mummy's bed for a cuddle. To be honest, she's been sleeping in my bed most of the time since my accident as she slept with my mum when I was in hospital (understandably).

Weak mummy I hear you say...

I have no excuses*...

I know...pathetic...I admit it!

* now I could use my accident, and go on about
  bones hurting, tired, crutches blah blah
  blah...but I don't really go for the sympathy
  vote! You've probably guessed that by now!

And I can't sleep. Just for a change.

"Insomnia...I can't get no sleep"...Faithless
1995....Feeling old too!

Anyway, my head starts going into overdrive...

The topic for tonight's insomnia:

I know I said this a bit earlier in the book but,
again, it's niggling at me.
I'm in total shock at the lack of humanity shown
by some people...there are people out there who
have been friends and/or family who have shown
no interest through myself whatsoever in whether
I'm alive or dead, or (less dramatically) how I am
following my accident.

Everyone knows about it, it's not been a secret. I
can only assume that people are really not
interested as they have their own lives to lead.

They haven't contacted me.

They haven't asked me about it.
They haven't written to me.
They haven't called me.

I had a broken body, not a broken voice or eyes etc!

Wow.

It's all I can say really, other than I hope that I will never be like that, or my daughter.

Rant over!

Maybe I'll doze off now...

Saturday 6th October - Puke

So, it has become very apparent, very quickly, this morning, that it is not an option to be unable to get to the bathroom quickly when your 4 year old is being ill! All they want is their mummy, and I couldn't get there for Iz...well, not in the time needed.

Thank goodness for grandmas!!

As a compromise, Iz and I spend the day cuddling on the sofa in between vomiting and sleeping. Bless her heart. I wish I was more mobile.

She is properly poorly. That's the only real time she'll sit still. And to be honest, I think it's only happened twice - once now, and once when she had chicken pox last February whilst we were in Dubai.

Sunday 7th October - Forgetfulness

So - drugs or accident?

It has to be one or other as, let's be honest, I had the memory of an elephant prior to all this.
I could remember anything, from a phone number to what we did on a weekend 4 years ago. I'd drive people mad with my excessive memory. No-one could ever win against me and they gave up trying.

So, how do I know I have a problem...

Well - there have been at least 2 conversations that I've had with people that I don't remember (one mentioned in here a while back with Neil).

And, in the last week, I have denied all knowledge of 2 business emails that it would appear I've had, read and have replied to.
In hindsight, on seeing them, I recognise that I've had them. But I couldn't tell you what I've done with them or what I was thinking at the time.
Ooops.

So, there is a problem for me.

It's MRI round 2 tomorrow. Let's hope it's the drugs and not the fact that the left side of my head has been tender to touch since the accident. I've realised that sadly it's not just a bruise as it's too long ago now for it to be that. The last of my bruises went weeks ago.

Anyway, back to today.

2 AMAZING things - as far as I'm concerned. Others less so!

The first:
I walked from my car and into Pete's with Iz, WITHOUT any crutches.

OMG! No crutches at all.

And I didn't look too much of a freak (I don't think).

I'm so proud of myself, and so was Izzy, which means the world to me.

Pete didn't even notice without prompting... typical man (sorry men that are reading this!).

The second:
On crutches this time....but I actually walked, in the sunshine, to Ellen and Jason's house.

Admittedly it's only 0.3miles, but it's a step (pardon the pun) forward for me.

I think I may sell the wheelchair.

I'll wait until I get my confidence that next Tuesday's operation won't have any negative impact on my mobility, but then it's going. I really don't see the point in having it as it's coming into winter, and it's only actually useful if we go for a long walk...
And I have to be with another adult so that they can push me.

Not Sarah.

Definitely not Sarah, not after the last time!! (sorry Sarah!)

Monday 8th October - Very chilled

I say very chilled as I have my MRI today, so I'm drugged up to the eyeballs on Diazapam. There's no way I'll be going into that tunnel otherwise!! The tunnel is done and it wasn't as bad as I thought, although I had my head locked in position...misery!
But, I managed to stay incredibly still which meant it only took 1 hour for the whole thing, back included...phew!

I get the results next week.

Hopefully there is nothing wrong with my head, but it definitely feels funny on the side. This is the side that has felt funny since 2 days after my accident...and probably since the actual accident, but I can't remember that bit.

And fingers crossed that the nerves in my back are just coming back to life, and not trapped by bone calcifying or anything...that would be unpleasant, and I don't like to think of the treatment...so I won't for now.

Tuesday 9th October - Next steps

So, big day.

Final operation. And some metal to come out.

I'm hoping for a few kilos to come off my weight, but Neil has pissed all over that by telling me that the metal implants are generally titanium and that it's one of the lightest metals there is.
Hmmm....I'll be lucky if it's a few grams!

Will have to switch to plan B for weight loss...will let you know when I know what that is and we can all become thin together!

Horribly early wake up at 0530....

It felt like I was off on holiday, but I very quickly remembered that I was actually in for my next op.

Off to Bristol we went.
0700 on the dot and I walk into Gate 21.

Southmead Hospital - seriously. If you haven't ever been there it's hard to imagine. But it's incredible. It's run to almost perfection, from my point of view anyway.

I was first on for my operation so the gown and stockings came out pretty quickly...beautiful.
I'm so glad Neil was with me to see me in all my glory (and to take photo's, which are not in here for obvious reasons)...but then I realised he's seen me in a much worse state!!

After asking 3 different people if I could keep the metalwork that is removed from me, and getting the same answer - no - I have resigned myself to the fact that I probably won't get it.
I'll settle for a picture of it though if Mr Acharya will take one after the operation - I hope he makes sure it's washed though!
I actually walked, no crutches, to the theatre. And then I was asleep again...hopefully for the final time from this hideous accident.

And boom...awake again.

General anaesthetics are weird...I can't explain it. You just lose time.

I walked to the theatre at 0911, and woke up back in my room at 1043.
They said my op (including all of the putting to sleep etc) would be 91 minutes...not bad timing then!

The pain.

Oh my goodness, the pain in my wound on the left hand side of my pelvis was incredible. I couldn't bend my leg towards me without it searing through me.

I've never felt anything like it. And I'm not being dramatic.

They gave me drugs, I've no idea what, I just took it.
It didn't touch it.
In the end they recommended I increase my daily tablets - up to 32 a day again then!

In terms of the general anaesthetic, I felt fine. No surprise there.

I'm totally odd and don't think I'm affected negatively by generals at all.

I had a cup of tea, 2 pieces of toast, and a flapjack. And then I wanted to go home. I got up, got dressed, and left by 1230!

The pain is just something I need to grin and bear for a couple of days I guess.

Neil drove us back to Cheltenham where we stopped off at Cook to get some food, and then arrived home where I proceeded to do the washing, sort the cat, tidy up, get the post, move the bins etc.

Pretty standard for me!!

And I wonder why people call me stubborn!

Neil doesn't say anything anymore - he knows better.

By the time Sarah arrived, the pain from my wound was almost unbearable. Thankfully she suggested some frozen peas and they actually took some of the pain away for a bit.

The night, unsurprisingly, painful.

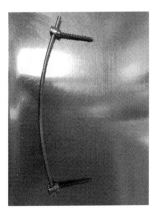

And this is the beauty that they took out....

Wednesday 10th October - walking!

I walked. Not just the walk around the corner to the coffee shop. I walked to the pub in the evening too. And home again.

WTF?! It's like something changed overnight! Taking that piece of metal out has had a great effect on my body.

I'm feeling good in myself too, which brings me onto the next thing...World Mental Health Day - today.

When I realised that this was today, I immediately went onto the BBC and The Daily Mail News websites...my 2 go to sites for the latest.

Neither of them had it featured anywhere.
I was gobsmacked.

Especially given all the work that the Royal Family
have been doing on this to publicise in the recent
months and years.

Anyway, I think it's important to shout about.
It's still the case that no-one talks about any
issues that they may have mentally.

What I find incredible is, that given everything
that I've been through with my accident and the
aftermath, not once since ITU have I been asked
about my mental state and if I need any support.
I say since ITU because one of the doctors, James
Roberts I think, said to me at one point that I
would probably need some help afterwards.

The crash was horrific.
The injuries are life changing.
The recovery is not quick.
And the repercussions are immense.

Nothing will EVER be the same. And no-one since that one occasion has mentioned any support for my mental health.

Wow.

And I'm a strong person.
So what if I wasn't so strong?

Thursday 11th October

The pain is not so good today...possibly the walking....I've probably overdone things again!

I tried to take it easy today. I'm so tired.
More than I've been since the accident I think.

Everyone keeps saying it's because of the general anaesthetic on Tuesday so I'll just listen to them and chill.
With the exception of picking Izzy up from school.
I'm going to surprise her and go in with no crutches...

It's fair to say she was surprised! And delighted!
She told everyone..even though they could
obviously see!

I collapsed when I got home again!

Friday 12th October - Proud mummy (and also 3 calendar months - which we ignore!!)

Iz's Harvest Festival at the school - it was
amazing. Probably because it's the first one for
me as a mummy!
Actually, being honest, the hall was a sweat pit
and it was hideous!
Next year I'll do what everyone else did and just
go for the relevant session!!

I took one crutch with me for the sympathy vote...
and to get a seat...it worked! Actually, I needed it
as I'm still can't stand up for long and the pain is
still there.

I got a bargain on my hair this afternoon - a colour
and cut for the price of a cut.

I'm in!

I fancied a treat, even though I can't really afford
it. I'm desperate to look better in myself.

On the way home I felt shocking...I just needed to go to bed. I called Neil and cancelled him coming over as I just needed to eat and sleep.

I was in bed by 1900. I think it might be a new record....for anyone!!

I actually slept too...until 0100 when I realised I hadn't taken my tablets. I took them and went back to sleep!!

Saturday 13th October - Bubbles Darling!

I woke up and rolled over.

Yes - rolled over!

Both ways!

Hooray!

It's a miracle in the making. I can roll over any way I want to and it doesn't hurt...too much!

My wounds from last Tuesday are a problem though - well, the left one is. I'm convinced there's something not right with it. I need to get it checked next week before I head off to the sunshine on Thursday.
Anyway, for now I won't touch it. Then it will be fine.

I did a bit of work as I have to spread it over the days at the moment.

I can't seem to manage a whole day still, not even half a day in one go. It's not really surprising, given what my body has been through, and all the tablets that I'm still hoovering up each day.

I also looked at my book (yes - this one!), and thought about needing a cover for it. So I've asked friends and family if they know anyone....we'll see if anything comes up for charity!

Actually, I've just realised that one of my cousins has some contacts...I will put the feelers out.
Neil and I actually spent the afternoon chilling in town. Reading the papers, writing this book, eating (lots), and drinking (bubbles). And all this was done before getting home in time for Strictly Come Dancing (my Saturday night viewing until Christmas!)...which I promptly slept through most of!
I'm seriously bad company at the moment. I can't keep my eyes open and I have very little of interest to say at all.

Oooh - the exciting bit that I forgot - as part of the Cheltenham Literature Festival which is on at the moment, JoJo Moyes was doing a talk at Hotel

Du Vin, where we happened to be sat for the afternoon....
And she was signing books afterwards....I didn't have a book, but I did have a post-it note!!
I raced downstairs to get a signature, and we had a bit of a chat. JoJo wished me luck with this book, so thank you JoJo!!

Sunday 14th October - Magic dust

Party time!

Not mine unfortunately....Izzy's cousin Lily.

Lily has turned 5 so we can have a big party to celebrate.

Both Lily and Iz seem to have become more clingy lately so neither of them wanted to participate at the start. Then poor Lily disappeared totally so Iz jumped in and became the magicians assistant. She would only do it though if mummy sat on the floor near her...so I got on the floor...

Hmmm...how the hell was I going to get up again?!

So - I tried the elegant (ish) way. That wasn't going to happen!

Chris (my cousins hubby) offered to help me, but I'm too stubborn for help as you've probably realised by now.

No - I'd rather stick my arse in the air and make a complete tit of myself in true Pringle fashion. And not in front of just a couple of close friends... we're talking 20+ strangers.

Perfect!

As a positive, once you've stopped laughing at me, I managed to be on my feet (with the exception of the aforementioned floor incident) from 12-4 with no crutches....yep, no crutches for 4 hours!

Amazing.

I'm actually seriously proud of myself.

But, on the drive home I can feel it.
My back is hurting, and my knee is hurting.

Mind you, I have the sorest of sore throats - which is seriously minor for me in the grand scheme of things - it's probably this that is making me feel rubbish.

Bless mum.
A lovely roast dinner was waiting for us when we got back. Iz went straight to bed (my bed, obviously) after demolishing her food, and I wasn't long after her!

But before that, there was something that really got to me tonight...

Part of my heading to Dubai this week, aside from getting some sunshine and TLC from the hotel staff, was to give my mum a break and to try and gt us back to a bit of normality afterwards.
She has been an absolute superstar throughout my recovery (I know we've had our moments), but I am on the up now, and I do my fair share. I cook. I do washing. I work. I drive. I sort bath time etc etc..

You get the drift.

So, when mum tells me that her friends in Chipping Norton feel the need to cook for her so as to look after her whilst she's back to rest next week, I felt (again) that it's a burden for mum to come over here still. I fully appreciate that this may have been the case during the last few months, but I fail to see it so much now.

I'm gutted as I want mum to be able to come over to see us, and not to feel that she has to do everything for us when she's here.

I think Mum knows that I'm upset as she's being super nice to me now.

I absolutely hate feeling like a burden...and I know that I harp on about we choose how we feel....!

Monday 15th October - germs

I feel horrendous.

How pathetic is it that a sore throat and a cough wipes me out so badly, when I've got the injuries that I have?!

Still, there's no amount of the lovely drugs that I'm on that will help my cough etc so I'd better just get on with it.

Iz off to school - tick
Doctors appt for the wound that doesn't feel good - tick

As predicted on Tuesday when I came out of the operation...the would on my left side is not right at all.
I went to the doctors to get them to have a look.

It's infected so I've got more tablets to add to my collection.
Joy - just add them to the pile!

So, no matter how much I try to get the number down, I still stay in the late 20's for tablets I take in every 24 hours for the time being

I have managed 3 days with half of the Tramadol dosage so far.
I don't feel brilliant, but I'm putting that down to the sore throat rather than medication…..
Will see how I feel tomorrow and make a call. If I'm still aching lots then I'll have to increase it again.

I have no idea why I'm pressurising myself to reduce my tablets. I guess I've always been the type of person that doesn't take anything. So to take tablets in any quantity for a prolonged period is an alien concept, and clearly not one that I am getting used to.

Also today - start of the week….

I received an email from my insurance company wanting to arrange to talk to me about the accident that the 3rd party are now claiming against me for.

Marvellous.

To be expected, but shite anyway.

There's actually nothing anyone can do until the official collision report comes out, and this could be up to 6 months.
It was a horrendous accident, of which I remember nothing.

We'll have to wait for the report then.

To be honest, I'm actually just glad that we're both still here. We both live to fight another day. And we're both as ok as can be expected after something like this.

After this I headed off to the hospital, again, to have the ultrasound of my cyst...you know...the one they found during the full body CT scan at the time of my accident.

It's never ending!

It's still there, but on the opposite side to the one that was in the report.

Great.

And I had to swallow the humiliation, that I felt, of having an internal scan too. But I still thought that this was purely down to me not drinking enough water prior to the scan.
I actually know now that it was so that the doctor could be sure about the cyst on my right ovary, not the left one as per thee initial report.

The poor doctor and nurse looked mortified at telling me. I think they felt sorry for me with everything that's happened.

Much appreciated, but I don't want anyone to feel sorry for me, I just need my health sorted ASAP.

So we are left with a question - did the 4cm cyst on my left ovary at the time of my accident go down on it's own, and one exactly the same size pop up by today on my right ovary?
OR did they tell us wrong information from the original CT in ITU 3 months ago?

Hey ho.

I'm seriously not going to worry. There's absolutely no point.

I'll wait until I speak to Mr Kaloo tomorrow.

It's going to be a good week!

Anyway when I got back I spoke to Tom at Aviva Insurance - he was lovely. He also had very little information, the same as me, about the accident. As I already knew, we need to wait for the full report to try and understand what happened.

That brings me onto the wonderful letter that I've received from the police offering me a Driver Alertness Course as a result of the accident.
I am having to accept the course but remind them that I have absolutely no recollection of the

events and that I'm only taking the course to avoid any potential penalty in the future.

Surely if something is so close, and there are proven to be no distractions or obvious causes, then it should be logged as an accident?

This was a horrible accident by all accounts.

Haven't we all suffered enough?

I just want to move on and rebuild my health.

Both of us who were driving will be in pain for life....and, together with us, our families too will never forget the events of 12th July 2018.

But I still stand by that we are both exceptionally lucky to still be here.

Tuesday 16th October - Au revoir

So, I always said that I'd wait for my final operation, and when I was walking...and then I would stop writing this.

So, I'm finished!

Or not as the case may be........

Given that there have been a couple of twists, I thought I would carry this on for another couple of weeks. Especially as it now has become apparent that I can't actually walk without crutches yet..boo.

I said I would write this until I was off them and walking freely again. Hopefully only another couple of weeks..and then I'll shut up and let you all read something else!

So...

After a relatively normal day working, I went to see Mark Silva for the follow up from my MRI last week.
He makes me laugh as he's got a really funny sense of humour...and I'm also eternally grateful to firstly him, and secondly Paddy Clarke...as they were the 2 that saw me in my 2nd worst state ever.
I say 2nd as I'm pretty certain I looked relatively bad just after my accident..but I'll never know!

I turned up in Mark Silva's office a couple of weeks ago in the worst pain I have ever experienced and he was the one who got Paddy to see me so urgently and sort it out.

Anyway...MRI....so my brain has got signs of trauma on it. The bottom back right. Subtle, but there.

It's apparently like a scar so will never go. I wasn't expecting this.

I went to see Mark about the left side of my head and it doesn't show anything, so Mark thinks it's bruising that might not go either. Like a scar again, but they don't go on the brain/head and can hurt for the longer term.

Marvellous.

Back to the trauma though...do I notice any symptoms?
No, but probably because of everything else (and the drugs) going on.

Brain trauma can cause various long term effects...memory loss, moods, change in behaviour, tiredness, changes in reactions, not wanting sex (what?!) etc.
It's not as simple as a broken bone, or other damage we may do to our bodies. It can't be fixed in the same way.

I've been referred to the brain unit at the Royal Gloucester Hospital as they are apparently amazing in this area.

I've had the letter...and the minimum wait is a mere 5 months. And that's been fast tracked by the consultant.
Mind you, I'll probably only just be able to walk properly by then so it's not that far away!

What I do know is that I have forgotten things since the accident.
And I also know that I am more blasé about things that happen in life.
Life is too short to get stressed about things, and about what might or might not happen to us and those around us.
I'm the first person to say that now.

I nearly lost mine on 12th July.

I still haven't faced into that.

Wednesday 17th October - stitches out!

I got to the docs very excited to be getting the stitches taken out of my last wounds.
No such luck!
Harriet took one look and said they weren't ready.
Bum it!

But then she told me that actually I'll be better off on holiday with the stitches still in.
And apparently I would have to wear dressings in the pool anyway.
So she gave me a load of waterproof dressings!

But, the real clanger was when she said "you have got a letter to state all of your medication to get into Dubai, and your injuries sustained from the accident?"

No! I bloody haven't! Do I need one??

Apparently so. Upon research - very late in the day I know - some of my meds are actually illegal in the UAE.
Balls.
Harriet got on the case for me.

Ok, so that's hopefully being sorted so off I trot to my physiotherapy appointment at the Winfield Hospital.
On the way there (thankfully) Harriet calls me to say that the doctor thinks my discharge form and the letters from the consultants would be better.
Thank goodness I'm going to the Winfield. Fingers crossed they can sort this whilst I'm there.

Today was always going to be busy, but now it's a nightmare

Physiotherapy was not remotely relaxing.

I've got new exercises, and a list of them to do in Dubai.

I'm progressing really well, but Fiona tells me that I'm not even halfway through my recovery.

That really hit me hard.
Harder than I think anything so far.

She also told me, in no uncertain terms, to stop trying to come off my medication. And to stop trying to reduce it. She said no one would expect me to be doing that yet and no wonder I've been in pain. She told me that I should keep it consistent until I see Mr Acharya in December.

I came away really subdued.
I don't know what I thought before about timescales. Or actually what anyone else thought.

To be fair, Neil reminded me that someone did say it would be at least a year to recover, to even a basic level, when I was in hospital.

I guess I just didn't really register.

And the walking without crutches was massive for me. I genuinely thought I was nearly there.

Ok, so I need to get back on it and think of all the positives, of which there are loads!
But everyone is allowed to feel a bit shitty sometimes, right?!

I actually didn't have time to feel rubbish. I head straight off to have my nails and eyebrows done...girly stuff for our holidays!

Thank goodness for driving again - it has literally saved me in the last few weeks. (Hospital appointments in Bristol, work, Iz at school etc) Obviously I'd have managed, but this makes it so much easier.

So, back to the girly things for holidays....they burnt my eyelids...again!
I definitely won't be getting my eyebrows waxed again.
I look ridiculous!

I headed home to pack, do some work, and cook some dinner for Neil.

That was the plan...

Reality...work done, packing thrown in, and Neil cooked for me!
We were in bed by 2200 as I had an early start at 0800 with Iz back.

I know, I know..."that's not early" ....

It is for me at the moment!

Thursday 18th October - Holiday!

Bye Jessie, and bye house!
Bye Mum!

Morning Izzy!
Thank you Pete for shutting my case and putting it in the car!

And we're off down to collect Sarah and to get to the airport.

Dubai...on crutches....

These things are great:
Straight through check in.
Fast track security.
Straight onto the plane.
Hardly any queuing whatsoever.

No upgrade though!

I must book more holidays whilst I'm on them to maximise some of the benefit

We got to hotel and had similar treatment due to the fact that I was hobbling somewhat. And Sarah was too because of her knee operation that she had just before the accident.

The facilities for the disabled are significantly better in Dubai than in the UK.
There are slopes everywhere, although I am trying to practise some stairs...physiotherapy instructions.
I've also been given mini squats and tiptoes to do.
We're keeping it simple for now and building some strength in my gluts and my right ankle.

Since finding out that I can't walk without crutches yet, we have gone a bit back to basics.

I'm going to try and forget about that bit on holiday....probably wrongly, but I'm sure it's not a massive surprise to anyone.

So rather than write a bit for every day, given that I'm sort of walking again, I thought I'd do some blocks of dates and then a summary of where I'm up to in life, especially given than I was planning to finish this book last week!

So - the holiday:

My pain has been bad for most of the holiday unfortunately. I've taken all my drugs, and at the right time. But it's still there, rearing it's ugly head.
From that perspective, I'm actually looking forward to going home and reducing the pain, hopefully.
See, Sarah and I realised that it's because there's actually quite a lot of walking to do on holiday. Clearly I'm going to context this with it being versus none, or very limited amounts of walking, at home!
Obviously there's generally not a huge amount to be done on holidays, but I've found myself going up and down to the room for things, taking Iz to the toilet, taking Iz to the ice cream bar, going to the main bar (for Sarah and I) - again, obviously.

So, we got to day 3 of 5 and I realised that I didn't have enough tramadol to get me through to mine and Iz's flight home on Tuesday, let alone the actual journey home too. Given that tramadol is my main pain killer at the moment, this is not an option for me. It's an illegal drug in Dubai so getting more out here is not an option either.
I did think about halving the rest of my doses so that I would have enough to see me through, but that would ruin the time we have here as the pain would be horrible.
The only other option was to look at an earlier flight home. It makes sense for us to get on the same flight that Sarah is on earlier in the daytime.

So, a certain airline....NEVER again.

Let me be honest, we've got on the flight..I'm typing this from the plane, so I'm clearly on the plane.
And they did take the change fee off my flight change.

But back to earlier...I had premium economy booked and paid for, on the return flight, as I need the space for my legs and pelvis. They tried to charge me c.£1,000 for 2 of us...for seats that I already had booked on the later flight!
As it is I've had to pay c.£250 for the 2 seats in economy.

They know that I need to fly for medical reasons as I've had to jump though hoops just to get on this flight (and it's nowhere near full!). I've emailed over prescriptions and a medical letter, together with the discharge form from the hospital to prove my case.

So, we get to the airport for the flight (in economy).
They haven't even sat Iz and I together. She's 4 years old FFS.
Oh, and it turns out that Premium Economy is overbooked. Can you imagine if I'd paid the incremental money and then been booted down a class anyway when we arrived to fly?!

As it is, they've managed to get us sat together, and made out that they'd done me a big favour in doing this.
We're together, at the back in economy.
On the wrong side of the plane for my bad leg to poke out.
And at a seat where my TV doesn't work.
And they don't have any food choice left as we're some of the last to get food.

I'm so hacked off.

Anyway, there are worse things in life! I've got on with writing this!

The holiday has been amazing, but tiring. Sarah has been great, but is also suffering with her knee (as I said) and her feet.

We made a right pair!
Am sure Iz will laugh with us about it when she's older...you should have seen us trying to get up and down the stairs together!

On our last night we found out that we could get golf buggies anywhere we wanted to go in the resort....we'd walked everywhere....typical!

Iz had a fantastic time and was an angel for the majority of the time.
Of course she refused to go to the kids club...even after doing a "pinky promise" on it. To be fair to her, she went on the first day for 10 minutes and then came out as she didn't like it at all. She's too shy for it apparently - her words!

So, not as relaxing as it could of been, but still good fun.
And Sarah and I got some work done on our business which is great.
We've both decided that we need to create more time in our schedules to focus on our business. And on ourselves.

It sounds so simple...but how many of us actually give ourselves time in our busy lives?

We had a testimonial from one of our current clients whilst we were away.
I am blown away by it, and it absolutely reinforces why I do it, and why we set the business up in the first place.

I love my clients, and they've all been amazing through this time where I've been recovering at the same time as working.
Thank you all if you're reading this!

Tuesday 23rd October - tears

After a long day - a flight home and then a drive back from Maidenhead to Cheltenham - Iz decides she wants to go to Daddy's tonight and not wait until the morning. That is absolutely fine with me as I just want her to be happy and she hasn't seen him for nearly a week. And it gives me a chance to get the washing done too!

What came next was not expected.

On the way home we saw an ambulance, and Iz
started crying. It was completely out of the blue
but not massively unusual for a 4 year old!

But then she started saying how she doesn't want
me to be hurting for ever from my accident.
She was distraught.
I've told her that I'm fine over and over, and told
her again today, but she has heard me say that
there will be pain at times and she doesn't want it
to happen.
She also told me how she cried on Pete when I was
in hospital because she was missing mummy.
It absolutely broke my heart.

I'm writing this now with a really heavy heart, and
it is truly broken.

My little girl means more to me than anything or
anyone, and it is hideous to see her so upset about
something that I can't make any better.

Equally I know there's nothing that I can do about
it other than be here for her now, and I also know
that she was in the best hands possible throughout
the time that I was in hospital. Thank goodness I
came home when I did, and didn't stay in hospital
the extra 2-3 weeks that I probably should have
from an injury perspective.

Wednesday 24th October - the eve of 15 weeks... from my mum

"15 weeks in the life of a mum. Is that all it is I ask myself, just 15 weeks since my precious daughter's life hung in the balance. It's been a long, tough road for us all, and I've never felt exhaustion like it. There were times when I collapsed on my bed at night in tears not wanting to go on, but somehow I found the strength to continue. The power of prayer! But what a remarkable recovery so far and I'm proud of the determination my daughter has shown in very difficult times. The pain has been, and still is, a major factor but she is now mobile. I can remember the weeks when movement was impossible, even getting to the loo was very difficult, now she is doing everything, well almost, and probably too much! We don't know what the future will bring but my darling granddaughter still has her mummy and I still have my beautiful daughter so life is good."

Final Chapter - so she said! (December 23rd 2018)

So - as time moves on and life progresses, I wonder where half of this year has disappeared to.

Oh yes, the sofa!!

What I also realise is that I seem to have missed out the half and half stage. I mean the middle stage here. The stage where I get my backside up and about, but don't do too much every day.

Nope, I've gone straight to full on every day, and suffice to say, I'm feeling like shite.
Apparently I shouldn't even be considering going back to work until the New Year, and full time work will be even later.

Hmmm....so (more than) full time work, plus being a mummy, plus building work, plus writing a book isn't such a good idea then?!

Work

So I'm not to work until February 2019.

Ha ha ha ha ha ha ha.

I'll just pick myself up off the floor from laughing

What I love is this notion that I can take time off sick. I am a single mummy, with a 5 year old daughter, and a mortgage, and bills to pay.

Oh - and I've been having to work since September just to keep afloat!

Being sensible, I've made the decision to leave 5th Season Fruit and focus on my health and my family with a bit more of my time.
Although it's an amazing brand and product, I can't give it the time it deserves at the moment and so I have to leave.

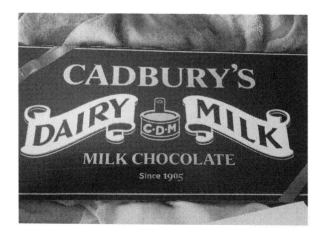

I am, however, going back to join one of my favourite companies of all time - albeit a slightly different one to what it used to be....
I'm heading back to see some of my old friends, and to work on one of my favourite accounts, with my favourite brands.
Good times.

Isabel/Being a Mummy

I could do without what is happening with Iz, as I'm sure she could too, but she is now the priority for me.

My gorgeous gorgeous Isabel, who was without her mummy for nearly a month, knowing only that her mummy had been in an accident and had hurt her leg.

And when she did finally see mummy after that initial 2 weeks in the hospital, she had a mummy who wasn't the strong role model she had seen her whole life so far.
I was in a hospital bed with a wee bag for goodness sake!

And when I returned home, which was meant to be exciting for everyone, I was actually a complete cabbage on the sofa for weeks:

Iz couldn't cuddle me properly.

She couldn't do the things she had done previously with me.
She couldn't go anywhere with me.
And she couldn't disturb me if I was asleep.

My poor little girl's sense of security, which was already dented massively by the separation of her parents, went out of the window totally.

And now it's mine and Pete's job to help her to rebuild it.

And we need to do that even with me not up to full speed.

We have to start it now as I am seeing strong effects of separation anxiety in her: it's impacting her at school, her sleep, and her wellbeing.
I can't have that, and I absolutely will not stand by and let it continue.

We had her first ever parents evening a few weeks ago. I was actually really looking forward to it as I was expecting to be told that my child is an angel at school etc...

We were told that Iz is their "worry" this year:

She is not as social as she needs to be.
Not as brave.
Not as secure in herself.

And so you see...

Don't get me wrong, in isolation I'd probably ignore it to an extent and just make a few tweaks to our lifestyle here and there.

But these are exceptional circumstances and I have absolutely no knowledge of the impact of something like my accident, especially not when combined with everything else.

I can do divorce...it's my business.
But the accident of a parent...nope, not a chance.

So I went to see a child behaviour specialist to get a better view.

Heartbreaking.

That's really all I can say.

I've sobbed a lot.
And I've argued with people a lot.
People don't always get it, they just assume that your child is playing up, but you know as a parent.

She's been through tough times in her 5 years. But what an amazingly tough cookie she is, most of the time.

When she's not, I see lots of heartbreaking things...

She can sob herself to sleep on me at night.
She still needs to sleep in my bed with me.
She needs to cuddle my hand to fall asleep.
She needs to sleep on a part of me all night.

She's terrified of the weather and the noise that it could bring with it - triggered by a loud clap of thunder a while back.
She's highly sensitive to noises, and wears ear defenders to school most days.
She has wet herself when it's been at it's worst.
She can stop eating if she's worrying too much about the weather.
She gets tummy aches a lot from her anxiety, we believe.
She is obsessed with checking the weather forecast - waking in the night to check it for the next day.
At it's worst, we had to check the weather app over 30 times in 3 hours one afternoon.

She needs and wants her mummy and daddy more than ever. She feels the safest when she's with either of us and this is just the reality that we're dealing with for now.
She needs stability and routine more than ever too, so Pete and I have agreed that we will not move nights around etc at the moment.

This is how Iz sleeps every night...so that you can see how deceptive a picture can be:

"Cute" I hear you say...

Not really - heart wrenching - look at her arms. One protectively over my body, and the other with the hand touching my face (off the picture).

But we'll get her better, it's our mission.

Drugs

I'm still on them!

16 tablets a day at the time of writing this (accident +23 weeks).

I actually asked the doctor in November - "how long would the average person be taking all of these tablets for following this severity of accident?"
I appreciate that there probably isn't that many of us, and that everyone is different..but I just needed some kind of idea...

A year.

A YEAR - average.

Wow.

I'm seriously going to stop trying to take myself of them for now (and yes I have still been trying this in various different ways, even though I've been told not to).

Here's what I'm still on:
Various painkillers - still the strongest dose of tramadol possible, plus the top level of gabapentin, plus paracetamol, plus venlafaxine for the anxiety.

What makes me laugh (not exactly laugh, but...) is that I even have to take tablets to neutralise the effect of all the drugs on my digestive system (read into that "pooh"!).

I've had various changes in medication over the past months, and in the brands supplied by the chemist, but none so bad as the new brand of tramadol equivalent they gave me last month.
The tiredness...exhaustion.
And the sickness.
And the sleepiness.
I couldn't eat.
I couldn't drive.
And, the best one, I couldn't sleep!!

Myself and the doctors have insisted on the old ones! The chemist have to order them in especially for me much to their disgust.

Seriously though, if that's the effects that people have to deal with when taking some brands, they should bin them and try another before saying that it's the wrong drug totally.
Anyone who is reading this and has to take them, just try a different brand. There are different effects on different people, and it's worth checking!

Being on all of these tablets and having a 5 year old sleeping in my bed are 2 of the most un-conducive things ever!

I need my rest, not legs kicking into my bad bones every 5 minutes!!

It's actually a bonus at the moment that Iz is at daddy's when she is....it's my sleep catch up time!

Injuries

They're still there too!

Although I've stopped my physiotherapy and hydrotherapy that I was doing bi-weekly, I'm trying to do it for myself at home. And the plan is then to go once ever couple of months to see Fiona and make sure that I'm making the right progress.

My right knee is probably my biggest worry physically...ironic really considering that it wasn't even injured during the accident.
Although it is where they went in on my right leg to input the rod in my femur.
Mr Acharya thinks there could be some nerve damage, so we're going to re-assess it at 1 year post the accident. It may need an operation, or may have cured itself.
I am continuing to build the muscles in both legs. And I am continuing to learn to bend my knees - which hurts like hell!

I rarely use a crutch now. Only if I'm in pain really.

My brain appointment should come through in the next few weeks and I can start to understand what impact the injury and it's scarring on my brain has had.
And then I can build this into my life and how I do things.

This is the one that is the hardest overall, as it's not visible…

I think I'm different with regards to food. It's just not important to me anymore.
Don't get me wrong - I eat - lots. And I'm not wasting away or anything, but it's very out of character for me to not be remotely interested in what I'm eating.

My memory is also shot to shite….
At first I didn't realise, but why would I?
Then it was what you don't know you don't know.
Then it was the tablets.
And now it's purely that my memory has taken a serious knock.

That's probably the crux of the matter. Not that I want to believe it. And it's subtle, sometimes more than others:

The odd birthday card here and there - have I sent one or haven't I?
Emails - "I didn't get it"…oh, yes I am copied in on it….hmmm….oh, there it is!
"I didn't say that" - yep, you did!

So I guess we'll see when I finally stop taking all my tablets, but as I continue to reduce them, the problem is still there. My fear is that it's a permanent problem, and is one that is only shown by the trauma on my brain via a scan.

But so be it, I'm still here!
I'll have to adjust, and people will have to understand.

My cyst turned out to be nothing sinister thankfully...after a couple of scares over November and this month, but all is good and back to normal.

Wheelchairs/Mountain Seats/Crutches

Well - 2 are gone!!
I love eBay!

Actually my wheelchair went for £70 vs the £90 I paid for it....I'm so sad that this actually excites me.

And just the crutches remain. I suspect that I'll have them here, on hand, for a while still. I think that will be the new norm.

It's still only just over 5 months since it happened.

The reality is that I should still be taking it easy. I shouldn't be out and about as much as I am. I should be resting every day. I should be swimming a few times per week. And I should be cycling regularly to build my muscles.

The reality is that I am months ahead of expectations, and this is my stubbornness coming through again. As long as it doesn't come and smack me in the face at any point then I'm ok with this!
Actually, it's probably worth mentioning here that I'm registering for a 5k run.

Yes, yes...I know....I'm not allowed to run again. But I'm not going to let a little thing like that stop me am I?!?

I'll probably actually walk it, given that I could never run anyway. But even to walk it would be a major achievement in under 12months since the accident.
I'm determined to continue to raise money for the amazing teams involved in my rescue and my recovery.

Family/Friends/Loved Ones

Yes - Neil and I are still together. We've been through far too much together to let anything in the world beat us now.
We're going to make it work whatever is thrown at us.
We'll help Iz get the support she needs, and we'll continue to build on the relationship between her and the boys, me and the boys, and Neil & Iz.

Meanwhile, Neil and I will continue to build on our relationship too.

Family and friends are all still amazing.
My mum continues to help me, especially with Iz.
Everyone continues their lives.

Everyone seems continually shocked when they find out how many drugs I'm still on. I guess it's understandable.
I can't really talk. I ignore my injuries and portray an image of being absolutely fine. I'm just aching a bit....

Christmas

So - here we are at another Christmas.
One which, to be fair, I'm exceptionally lucky to be able to enjoy. Well, I will once I've got rid of

the disgusting stomach bug that I seem to have at the moment. Pesky kids and their germs!

Anyway, Christmas....a time of goodwill, merriment, and spending time with our family and friends.
A time where most of us stop for a few days and enjoy the break with our loved ones.

But not for some. Not everyone has a happy time. Not everyone has family or friends to be with. And, sadly, not everyone makes it through the year.

And importantly to remember, accidents still happen, no matter what day of the year it is. Our amazing NHS are still needed, as are our emergency services - both probably more than ever. Blood donations are still used. And operations still happen at all hours to save peoples lives.

There are teams of people working around the clock every single day of the year to ensure that as many of us as possible remain safe and here until our time is truly up.
My time wasn't up this year, and for this I am eternally grateful to all of those involved in my rescue and recovery.

Being sat here tonight it really hits me how hard these teams work, how dedicated they are, and how we really should remember how lucky we are.

I'm not sure I will ever truly believe, or think about, the full extent of how serious the events of Thursday 12th July 2018 were.

And, although I can walk again (albeit with a bit of a hobble), there are still loads of other things going on - the brain trauma to find out more about and manage, more testing on the pains in my back, the repercussions of the accident on my loved ones - Iz in particular, house extensions, work....and so the list goes on.

But this is just life.

We all have things to deal with, and we take them in our stride, we make choices associated with them. And we choose how to let them effect us.

I will continue to laugh lots.

Continue to play lots.

Continue to have accidents - hopefully not as horrific as the last one.

I will continue to make mistakes, and I will continue to get both good and bad news.

But, it's up to me to choose how I respond and handle things. I make my own success, be it physical or mental.

So - to everyone out there who agrees with me: Hold your head up high, and be strong, it helps you immensely!
And remember, life is good and is there to be enjoyed, no matter what is thrown at you.

Lots of love to everyone reading this, and thank you for helping me to raise money for the amazing people that saved my life on Thursday 12th July 2018.
A day etched on my mind forever.

Happy happy Christmas to all my friends and family - you are truly amazing and I wouldn't have made it through this year without all of you!

And bring it on 2019 - you can't top 2018!!

Final Chapter - this is (most definitely) it (September 2019)

So a year down the line, and wow....what a year it's been. To be honest, it's been a total rollercoaster of emotions.

I started it by being involved in an accident that nearly killed myself and another driver...and that was just the beginning of a journey, for me and those that are close to me.

A lot of the feedback I've had on this book, since the launch in February, is that it leaves readers needing answers. Answers that I either didn't have when I originally wrote this, or couldn't write about at the time of publishing a few months ago.

A year on from the accident and a lot has come to light, a lot has been resolved, and we're all a lot better physically than we were this time last year.

One of the biggest things for me has been to find out that it was actually Midlands Air Ambulance that lifted me and got me to Southmead Hospital in time for them to work on me. I believed, for almost a year, that it was someone else. So when I say it's been a rollercoaster, this is just one example!

Back in April I made the decision not to pursue any claim on the insurance companies involved as I decided that both my health and Isabel's health were more important. The money wasn't a driver for me and I wasn't interested in this causing anymore bad feeling. It had been shown, as part of the investigation, that my car was over the line in the middle of the road. We didn't know why, and because I had no memory, at the time, it was impossible to try and provide a reason. No one was prosecuted or charged with any offence.

For me, life isn't about money. I'm just grateful to still be here. Although, in my current situation a bit of money would be helpful!

Anyway, back to the events of the year:

Recently Neil and I had the pleasure of attending the Midlands Air Ambulance Charity annual fundraising ball. I can honestly say that it was the most inspiring event I have ever been to.
Some of the people that were there...survivors (thanks to the amazing efforts of the team), air ambulance paramedics, pilots, call desk teams, fundraisers, family and friends of both survivors and, sadly, those that haven't survived (but have been helped by the team), and the list goes on. There were tables of companies there that donate over and over to keep these guys going.
Oh, and I got a hug with Will Mellor - my claim to fame!

Midlands Air Ambulance are one of 9 Air Ambulance charities in the UK. They are solely funded by donations and get absolutely no government funding....yet they are out there saving lives (like mine) daily.

They need to raise over £9m per year at MAA to keep their 3 aircraft in the air and all the cogs running behind the scenes.

Each "mission" costs them £2,500+ to run.

So I made a pledge on that night at the ball.

I pledged the following:

"I will write a final section to my book of a year down the line, and I will republish once this is done"

And here we are - in the midst of writing...

This is Neil and I on the night of the ball -
beautiful weather and a fantastic group of people!

And here goes with some detail...

I look fine....you'd never know what happened a
year ago....except for those times that I get a
shooting pain up from my right ankle...I can go
pretty pale then so I tend to sit quietly for a while
to stop myself being sick.
Oh, and towards the end of each day, when I look
like a 80 year old trying to get out of a chair...
So, you'd definitely be forgiven for not even
realising what had happened 12months ago on that
fateful day.

And I also have to remind myself that those
around me probably forget about it too, on the
surface...you'll all know by now that I'm
exceptionally stubborn so I was back on my feet
way ahead of any predictions, and I have tried to
live as normal a life as possible since then - not
least of all for Isabel as that's what she's needed.
I made a choice a long time ago that I will not look
for sympathy and I will get on with whatever is
thrown at me, to the best of my ability.

I've been without my crutches since November 18,
so I actually only used them for 4 months or so. To
be honest, I needed to get rid of them as soon as
possible because, as I eluded to, poor Iz couldn't
stand to have them in the house. For her,
normality needed to return as soon as possible,

and mummy on crutches was certainly not normality for her.
I can't run or do anything sudden that involves my legs* (in particular my right), feet or pelvis...and this is likely to be the case for the rest of my life....bang goes those Zumba classes and those marathons I was going to run.
Ok, so I was never actually going to run a marathon....I can't even run to the chippy!

So, although running is not my thing, its one of the lifelong complications that I have now, and there are others too.

But I'm still here! And that's the main thing to remember.

*in case you were wondering, I can still have sex!

So I could spiral into a depression about the potential lifelong impact of my injuries, but to be honest I don't feel like there's any point.
This is purely my choice, and I totally understand that we're all different and handle things in our own way. But I've chosen to deal with things if and when they happen, rather than worry about things that may or may not happen in the future.

I'm living in the here and now.

I could get stressed about the past, or have anxiety about the future....but what's the point? It's a drain on my energy!

Now, the other injury that I have, which I actually had to google to see if it's classed as physical or mental...is my brain injury.

It's physical apparently.

As I wrote about back in October, I have a brain injury on the lower right hand side of my brain. The effects of this are still coming to light as I'm still on various medication and it can be hard to know what is caused by this vs injuries, but I've had a stab at the effects for some friends recently as a couple of people asked me to explain given that you can't see them...

I'm actually trying to deal with it at the same time as PTSD, so the effects are all mixed up...but here's my experience of   My Perfect Storm as I now call it:

My Perfect Storm

Brain injury and PTSD colliding...sometimes invisible injuries are much worse than the physical ones...

- I get little or no sleep every night
- And when I do, I have vivid dreams and nightmares
  - so vivid from the previous day activities/conversations that I have to write down what has actually happened daily and refer to it to check what is real vs not real
- I cry - a lot
- I forget what I'm saying mid sentence, and it doesn't come back
- I mix my words up - known as "mummy's funny word moments" in our house
- I forget names
- To be honest, I forget everything really!
- Lists are good!
- I'm tired ALL the time... so unbelievable tired ...I need to rest every couple of hours for a couple of hours, otherwise I'm sick
- I'm numb - not physically, but mentally...so people probably think I don't care, but I do...a lot
- I think that people are against me all the time
- I feel guilty constantly, even if there is nothing to feel guilty about
- I rarely go out, and if I do it's very early if an evening
- I'm in bed by 9pm most nights
- I rarely socialise with anyone other than 1 or 2 that see me day in day out
- I constantly mess things up - burn toast, too much washing liquid, shampoo etc...
- I try to clear the decks constantly ...and quickly...so, again, people think I don't care..but I do
- I still need my mum to help me A LOT - she's a superstar!
- I need A LOT of cuddles from Iz - she's a superstar too!
- Basically, at the moment, I do what I need to to survive and to look after my little girl...and that's it in a nutshell...for now!

But I'm still here!! And that's why this won't beat me...and I will keep raising awareness for all the things that no one talks about x

Oh, and I'm STILL on the blasted tablets!!
At least I've managed to reduce them significantly….45 per day in July 2018 to 4 per day now. I'm still on some pretty strong ones, including a high dosage of Tramadol. But I have removed the Gabapentin (also strong), and reduced the Tramadol by 25%. And I stopped the Morphine last September, so pretty soon after the actual accident.
It's really hard to tell what is an effect from the medication and what is actually a permanent feature in my life, as mentioned previously.
But rather than focus on this, I've had to come to terms with just accepting it for what it is right now.

Life is here and now, as I mentioned.
My life consists of a brain injury, PTSD, PLUS medication…and that's what I have to build my knowledge around.

You'll be unsurprised to know, given that I'm so stubborn, that I've tried to reduce my medication down numerous times…it took me 3 attempts to come off the Gabapentin earlier in the year. It's a controlled drug that can be difficult to take away and you have to do it very gradually…and, of course, your body has to be ready. Your injuries have to be at the stage that your body can be without the medication.
I finally reached this point in April.

And it's the same for Tramadol...and my body tells me that I can't get below the level I'm on for now. When I spoke to the doctor about this recently, he told me to stop trying. He highlighted the fact that my body is full of metal that is not meant to be there in how our bodies are designed...so it's no great surprise that it needs the pain relief.

I've had to tell myself that it's an amazing result to be where I am, and that it would be perfectly acceptable to be on prescribed medication for years.
So I'm going to stay as I am for the next couple of months (I'll probably need reminding of this in a couple of weeks as I'm sure I'll try to reduce things again!).

In terms of movement of my body, I can't walk more than about 1.5 miles in one go on any one day...slowly...and it gives me serious repercussions for days afterwards - ankle, leg and pelvis. Swimming and cycling are the best for me as there is no weight going through my pelvis.
So I swim when possible, and I have my bike that I am starting to use regularly.

I have actually gone for the crazy idea of doing a charity bike ride on 29th September this year. I am going to cycle from my home in Charlton Kings, to Strensham Airbase and see the crew that flew me to Southmead Hospital in Bristol on 12th July 2018. It's only 17 miles but, given what's happened to my body in the last 12 months, it's a long way for me and will be a massive achievement.

I'm doing this in order to raise vital funds for Midlands Air Ambulance.

So far I've raised over £800 for them, and I'm hoping to raise well over £1,000. This will be my first major fundraiser for them, and I will plan more!

I'm also starting to do volunteering work for them where I can - the first event for me was last weekend when they had their Strensham Airbase open day.

It was THE BEST day I've had in ages. So inspiring to meet so many amazing people. All of the crew were there from most of the shifts. The air ambulance went out to help 3 accidents whilst we were there, and the crew on duty still managed to participate in some of the events of the day. They also launched a brand new critical care car, to add to the one that they already run in the area. And BBC Midlands Today covered the story on the news that evening.

It was a hugely emotional day, not least of all when the air ambulance was taking off to go and hopefully rescue someone...that was me last year.

I caught up with some of the fabulous people that we met at the charity ball a couple of months ago - Katie, Dexter, Tim, Kerrie, Shane, and the list goes on. I have to call out Dexter - he is 6 years old and fundraises for MAA regularly. He saw them working on saving his grandad a few years ago and has tirelessly supported them ever since, together with his amazing mummy, Katie.

And then there's Tim, who gives up literally all of his spare time to support these guys. Tim is a DJ in his spare time so regularly hosts these open days, and he also supports them massively on social media and through other events.

And my final call out is to the lovely Helen, who works directly for the charity. Helen has been amazing ever since the day in April that I found out that it was actually Midlands Air Ambulance that lifted me. I had been under the impression that it was another charity before this. Helen took me into the MAA family and we have worked together ever since. Helen has been super sensitive to me and the situation, and always manages to judge things spot on!

These call outs could go on forever as the list is so long, and my not mentioning individuals in particular is not any reflection of how much they have also had an impact on me...all of the people and teams at MAA are amazing, I literally love them all.

Talking of best days, another standout one in the last few months was in May when I had the absolute pleasure of meeting Karl.

Karl was one of the blood donors whose donations saved my life on 12th July 2018.

The NHS Blood service called me and asked me if I would be prepared to meet one of my donors as part of the National Blood Week this year....I was totally up for it as it all helps to raise awareness for something that saves lives.

Did you know that 1 donation of blood can save up to 3 adults? Amazing huh?

Anyway, meeting Karl was part of a fantastic day that Neil and I had in Birmingham. Neil and Karl both donated blood on that day, on camera, and we met a lot of the team from the Blood Service.

It turns out that Karl is a graphic designer, so the new cover that you have this book in is courtesy of him! Thanks Karl!

From a mental health perspective:

To be honest, the last 12 months have been a complete head ****.

To have no memory of something, that you are blamed by a lot for, is truly horrific. I've always said that I can't think of anything worse than being accused of something that you haven't done...this is up there and, I believe, worse.

I've had to tell myself that, although I can't remember all of the specifics, I am a very competent driver and there would have to be a reason for my car being where it was, over the white line in the middle of the road. We know that there were no distractions such as drink/drugs/mobiles involved, but that's it.

The good news is that my memory is starting to return and I am clearer on what happened....the bad news is that there's not a great deal I can do about it now. But, it does help to have some clarity and to know that there was a reason.

The brain injury that I've said about started being looked at in April of this year so as to give me a chance to reduce my medication significantly first. Again, I had great news here that the injury I had sustained could get better.

With time and space.

There's the issue....time and space when you're self employed and trying to support a house, child, business etc is tricky.
So I had to make a choice that I would take a break from work for 6 months from June 2019. This was really hard for me. I'm a worker. I love to work. Weird I know!
I couldn't imagine not working....you'll remember from earlier, that I was back to work within 2 months of my accident. This is me, and that's my style. But I was paying for it and I had to make the call to take a break, for my future health.

So, the plan was to finish the contract that I was on with Mondelez, and then to take a break from the end of June.

But all this changed when I got diagnosed with PTSD towards the end of April.
I was signed off immediately.

I can honestly say that I had no idea what the impact of this was and would become as time passed.

Both of these things, at the same time, has been really hard to even get my head around. I haven't even started to deal with them yet (at the time of writing).

On that, I am starting treatment for PTSD next week. I'm having to do this privately as the wait on the NHS is over 9 months, and I really need to progress treatment now.

One of the reasons that I'm so keen to sort things out in my head, is that I broke.
Properly.
About 2 weeks ago.

I've "broken" once before in my life - in 2006. At the time I was covering 3 jobs and pretty much working 24/7. I had a complete breakdown and fell apart. I had to stop. I lost loads of hair - alopecia. I lost a lot of weight - there are better ways to do this.
And I vowed never ever to let it happen again.

So a lot of barriers have gone up in the last 13 years, for self preservation.

Anyway, a few weeks ago Neil and I split up for good. Times had been so up and down for the months since my accident and we weren't finding the route through before something else went wrong for us. Neither of us could do it anymore, it was making each of us ill. I guess love doesn't conquer all in the end.

I've realised in the last month since this that my accident and the repercussions from it have had such an impact on the relationship that we enjoyed.
We went from one thing to being something completely different overnight - Neil became a "carer" for his girlfriend, and I became more of a burden than a partner.
I became snappy, short fused, tired, intolerant, obsessive but dismissive at the same time, numb to feelings, and very quick to judge. I put him through hell if I'm really honest with myself, and I can't do that to anyone, let alone the person that I love and thought I was going to spend the rest of my life with.

So, sadly, we've gone our separate ways to spend some time focusing on ourselves and our families. And to try and have a hassle free life for a while, it's been really intense for the last 12months.

To top it off, a few days after we'd split up, I had some early symptoms of pregnancy. You see I've been here more times than I care to remember and recognise the signs for me - at least 6 times now.

Isabel is a miracle baby. After 4 miscarriages and 3 rounds of IVF, having to take steroids and other drugs for most of my pregnancy, bleeding all the way through, and various stints in hospital etc..she really is my little miracle girl.

This was unbelievable timing, and obviously not planned. And even more traumatic for me as I know all too well what happens in a pregnancy with me. My body can't carry them. I have an over active immune system which needs medically dampening down to be able to carry a pregnancy. So even if I was to find out I was pregnant (the 2 tests I did that day didn't show it), I was relatively confident that I would miscarry. The sadness of this for me, even though it would have been a nightmare situation, was that it would be a piece of myself and Neil and our happy times.

It was just sods law that I was now newly single from Neil, at the time where I needed him most for a hug and some support.

A couple of days passed and the symptoms were still there...annoyingly. I did a test again, and it was positive.

Great.

The timing was so inappropriate for telling Neil, but I felt it was the right thing to do, he would want to know. My amazing friends rallied around to give words of wisdom in the absence of a partner to lean on.

But for me, I knew what was going to happen in my heart of hearts...be it in a few days, weeks, or months.

And sure enough, a couple of days later, the bleeding changed and got heavier.
There goes the miscarriage then.
The doctors confirmed it for me, and a couple of days later I got the negative test. Another one to add to the list.

On the plus side, it was in time for my friend Ellen's 40th party, so I could enjoy some champagne after all. To be honest I felt like I deserved it after the last 10 days.
Now I could try and move on from my relationship, and so could Neil.

The realisation of the whole situation, and my behaviour's impact on things with Neil and I over the last 12 months, completely floored me. I'd spent over 2 weeks crying at the split and the pregnancy/miscarriage, and then I just fell apart completely when everything around the impact of my PTSD on my behaviour was highlighted to me on the Thursday night.

But I did make a decision that night. And that decision was that I couldn't continue to feel like I had been. I needed to get myself sorted properly, for myself and for my little girl. I couldn't continue to cry every single day like I had been. I couldn't continue to feel like my heart had been ripped in 2.

I wrote to Neil to try and explain, which is hard to do when you don't really understand yourself. I hope he can start to understand and to feel a bit better about some of the things that have happened.
I went to the doctors the next day to balance my medication and to try and understand some of the broader impacts of the things that I am taking - they mess with your head too.
And I booked myself in for PTSD treatment from next week.

The next day I stepped up the training for the bike ride, and I threw myself into all the good things that are going on for myself and Isabel, because I'm very clear that there are a lot of them and I need to be focusing on those rather than the negative things that have happened.

And Isabel, what a superstar. My absolute mini-me. She's been on such a journey in the last year. I hate thinking about what I've put her, and others, through. But equally, I see how phenomenally strong she is for a 5 year old. She has been through more in her 5 years than most go through in their lives...and she's still the happiest little

bean ever. She makes me smile ever single day. She makes me laugh all the time when she's with me - well, most of the time...I do get cross with her too occasionally!
She makes me feel even more grateful for still being here.

I wrote about the anxiety she had been suffering. She started play therapy in January of this year, and still goes once per week now. It's been her absolute saviour. And her school have been a fantastic support for her, putting in all sorts of measures when she needed them.
She still suffers, especially if routine is thrown out of the window. The summer holidays were hard for her, but the transition into year 1 at school has been good as it's given her back the routine that she needs so much.
She's still sensitive to noises, but not as much. It just depends on how much is going on for her.
And she still gets anxious about the weather at times. Again, it just depends on how "full" her mind is.
The school think that all of the loss and change she's suffered in the past few years has built up and triggered the anxiety, so we're going to review things again in the new year to check that things are continuing to improve.
If I'm really honest, I suspect that she is very slightly autistic. As I say though, very slightly. And we'll see as time progresses.
What really matters is that she is a happy little girl.

She's secure and knows how much she is loved, and she's building her confidence as she becomes less anxious about things.

She's my world.

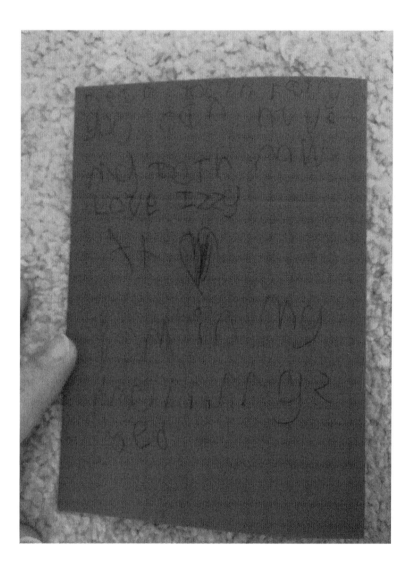

So, where am I at now?

Well, all of the "break" for me was only a week or 2 ago so things are still very raw.

But life is good.
My friends and family have been amazing.
Isabel has lost her first tooth this week and wrote this to the tooth fairy tonight, melting my heart at the same time:
You see, I have so much to be grateful for in life.

I'm still here for a start!

I have a beautiful little girl. I have a mum who is my absolute rock and who supports us no end. I have fabulous friends - both old and new. I have a gorgeous house in a great town. I have a brilliant wider family. I have a great business to expand in the future where I can help others.
And I am now a very real part of an amazing new family too - Midlands Air Ambulance.

This book is all about making tough choices in life, the pro's and cons of being both determined and stubborn, being thankful for what we have, and just getting on with it.

But what it's really here for, is to raise vital funds for the Midlands Air Ambulance Charity. Each and every book sold (whether paperback or on kindle) has a profit, and every penny of this profit goes to MAAC.

That is my commitment to them, and my way of starting to say thank you.

Thank you for looking after me. Thank you for being there for me. And thank you for getting me to the hospital in time for them to save me, so that I can still be here to see my little girl grow up. To hug her on nights like tonight. And to get excited with her about all the things that you should do with your children - like the tooth fairy tonight!

So, please, write a review of this book to keep it in the best sellers chart and to keep it raising funds for a charity that saves lives, every day of the year.

Big love from me to you and your families. Hold them close, and be kind to one another, always x

Printed in Poland
by Amazon Fulfillment
Poland Sp. z o.o., Wrocław

49331105R00181